How To Write Evocative Poetry

A Guidebook For Unlocking Creativity, Expressing Truth & Captivating Imagination

Zachary Phillips

ISBN: 9798850009748

3

Introduction

In my opinion, writing evocative poetry is part magic, part science, and part practice. All three of these components need to be in place if you want any hope of your words moving anyone.

The magic comes from deep inside. It is the connection between disparate thoughts, the spontaneous 'ah ha' moment, the revelation, the whispering on the wind. It is the ethereal muse desperately hoping to work though you to bring its vision to life.

You my dear poet, cannot control the magic, you can only harness it. You can only open yourself up to it and allow it to flow through you. You may get the accolades from the creations that it inspires, but in this one part, you are not totally in control. You can cajole inspiration, you can expose yourself to media, you can sit in silence, you can do any number of things to hear its call. These actions work, and I will share some in this very book. But ultimately the muse chooses and if it chooses you, you better damn well be ready.

The science of writing is probably the easiest part to learn. It is the technical advice, it is the observation of patterns, it is looking at what works and asking why. It is study. There are countless resources on this topic, and I share with you what I believe to be the most important things you need to know here as well.

Practice is the most important aspect of the process. You can have all the inspiration in the world, along with limitless theoretical knowledge of how to use an endless number of tools, but until you have done the work, so many times as for it to become second nature, all of that is useless. **Practice will turn mediocre into magnificent.** You will lean the artistry behind the science and the intersection of magic throughout the entire project. You will discover intangible nuggets of wisdom, both about the craft, and about yourself – then you will learn how to apply that knowledge into your work.

So, be open to the magic, study the science, and practice what you have learnt. Simple enough, but most writers I have spoken to neglect one of the above pieces, and it shows in their writing. **Without magic, it is uninspired. Without science, it is unfocused. Without practice, it is scarce.**

It is the last group that really upsets me on a fundamental level. I have read amazing poems from potential masters of the craft - works of art that fundamentally floor me. But unfortunately, when I enquire further, I am loathe to discover that it is their only piece, or one of a very small selection of finished works. What a shame for the world to have their genius and ability hidden. I cannot help but feel that with practice, these poets could produce such quality en masse. Perhaps they are afraid of failure, or lack the self-belief, or don't have the time or drive to push forth and practice their craft. Either way, I feel like I am missing out, and will no longer stand for such a travesty.

Of course, the same holds true for the other two groups as well. The poet who lacks magic, can produce and is technically competent, but adding a touch of magic would make their prolific work shine so brightly that it risks eclipsing the true masters. And for those without science, they need to just spend a little time studying their craft, and their natural ability and drive will intuitively latch onto the concepts presented to them and the quality of their work to also rise.

I often tell other poets that they are naturally more gifted than I. Their poetry is raw, powerful, and moving. But ultimately they lack something. Something that I have. Perhaps it is self-belief, or drive, or fortitude, perhaps it is technical knowledge or an understanding of how to capture the magic, maybe it's time spent studying the craft. Regardless, it is truly a shame, because I honestly think their work is better than mine – if only they would actually write more of it! Their best piece may beat mine, but I hold the next 99 slots on the ranking list, and eventually I will claim that first spot as well.

I don't want to, but I will, because I write. And so can you. This book will show you how to access the magic, will teach you the science, and convince you to practice. It will help you through your blocks and get you to put words on the page. It will guide you when you doubt and encourage you when you need it. Put simply, **if you work with this book, this book will help you to write evocative poetry**. Poetry that will move you and, if you choose to share it, the world.

Part 1: What Is Poetry? - Will contextualise the conversation, clarifying exactly what a poem is, as well as provide insights into the creative process as well as my journey as a poet.

Part 2: Creative Advice - Will help you to turn off the internal editor and start writing. It will get the words out of your head and onto the page, it will show you how to open yourself up to creativity and give you tools to express what comes. It will suggest different ways to inspire yourself and provide some guidance on how to play in a way that fosters true expression.

Part 3: Technical Advice - Will help to make your poetry pop. You will learn how to reduce the clutter, polish your work, and how to edit it to a publishable standard. This section covers the tips, tricks, and concepts necessary to take your poetry to the next level.

Part 4: Writing Activities - Contains a collection of activities that will boost your creativity and enable you to write amazing poetry. It is a toolbox that can be used when needed; to inspire, troubleshoot, or move past any creative blocks hampering your ability to get words onto the page.

Part 5: Worked Examples - Will take you behind the curtain of the creativity process. You will see the initial seeds of a poem and how it transformed over time, from conception to completion.

Part 6: Resources - consists of a collection of books, podcasts, talks, and other guides that you can use to take your writing even further.

This book is over 35,000 words long. Whilst this length is justified, it is possible to condense it all into a single sentence summary, one that if implemented, would take you further than anything else you will discover in this, or any other, book.

"If you want to learn how to write evocative poetry, read and write every day".

That's it. Just write and read every day and your poetry will improve. How can it not? You are both practicing and studying the craft. If something moves you, ask yourself why. If something stands out as interesting, figure it out. Look for patterns. Question the text. Determine why you liked one piece of work but not another. Then practice implementing what you have learnt, comparing your current poetry against your past poetry, and the poetry of others, investigating what works and what doesn't.

From the onset I want to make it clear: I am self-taught. This doesn't mean that I have lived a cloistered existence where the poetry somehow just naturally sprung forth from my inner world and onto the paper. No. All that means is that I haven't formally studied creative writing, literature, or poetry at a university or college. I did what you are doing right now. I discovered creative people that I connected with and read their work. I searched far and wide for the best resources and consumed them. I practiced what I learnt and compared my creations to the best in the field. I kept reading and I kept writing.

The results speak for themselves; multiple poetry collections receiving number 1 new poetry releases, 5-star ratings, glowing reviews, and an ever-increasing following for my work across social media, website, and podcasts. The more I write, the more people are resonating with my work. That said, the goal of my poetry is never to 'sell' – that is just a pleasant by-product. My goal is to express myself, completely, fully, and effectively. The better I am at wordsmithing, the better I can express myself.

One of my fears is that people look at my writing and get intimidated. Or more specifically, begin to doubt their own abilities. Hundreds of messages and conversations have confirmed this fear. Time and time again, I find people comparing their words with mine – then feeling like they come up short. But it's a false comparison. **When I compare my words to others, I feel like I am the one that comes up short. Why? Because I can never write like they** can. I don't have their voice. I don't have their experiences. I didn't live their life. Thus, if I tried to write like them. I would fail. What's more, I am far more critical of anything I do — whereas, I can immediately appreciate the beauty in another work. The artist's curse!

Whilst it would be beneficial not to compare your work to others, as to not crush your ego, and thus dissuade you from writing, doing so would also limit your ability to learn from others. Walking the knife's edge between healthy comparison and harmful self-criticism is a learnt skill - one that comes with practice. You may not even be comparing yourself to one person, but against a body of work. You may feel stale, like it's all been said before, or that you have nothing new to add. Perhaps, but just know that it hasn't been said by you yet. **Nothing is unique under the sun, but how you speak about the commonalities of the human condition will be.**

This book will take you behind the scenes and reveal to you some of what I'm trying to do. I am a teacher by trade, I taught high school for over ten years, and have been teaching or coaching in other fields ever since. I like to give people a combination of technical skills and overarching concepts or principles to slot those skills into. Basically, I will give you the tools, and suggest some guidelines of how to use those tools to write evocative poetry.

The best art you will ever do will likely come

from the depths of your soul, inspired by the most poignant memories, contrasted against your hopes, dreams, desires, shame, and core let downs. Thus, it is imperative that we combine the process of learning how to write evocative poetry with the appropriate inner work to enable ourselves to both look at, and heal from, the darkness of our existences. I have written extensively elsewhere on self-care, self-improvement, and self-help, so I won't dwell on it much here beyond the suggestion that whilst you don't *need* to do the inner work to be able to write evocative poetry, delving into the darkness and exposing your inner demons to the light will certainly yield some powerful poetry potential. I plan on writing a companion book to this one called 'Creative Writing For Healing', where I will go in-depth on how, when, and why poetry and writing in general is an effective method of healing, so stay tuned, and it may already be out! But until then I want to suggest that if you are struggling, do the work: see the therapists, implement the self-care, take the meditation if needed, and make the appropriate lifestyle changes – but also consider that the act of writing itself can be healing, in and of itself.

This is my motto:

The page listens, it doesn't judge, it has a perfect memory, yet can be discarded, it is practically free, is always available and has no preconceived notions. It will not interrupt you and can be discarded without consequence. So write. Write without judgement, filter, or planning. Write whatever comes, as it comes. Write until you have nothing left to say.

A note on format and presentation of this book. To make each section as clear as possible, I have chosen to reprint each poem that I am talking about, just after the discussion about it. This way you can easily see what I am getting at without having to flip back and forth between sections of the book to see the lesson in action. The downside of this approach is that some of the poems appear more than once in the text. This cannot be avoided, and on balance, I decided that the ease of reading supersedes aesthetics and length.

Finally, I want to pre-emptively address some potential confusion. The astute reader will quickly realise that I seem to fail to take my own advice, and in many cases do the exact opposite of what I am telling you to do.

This is intentional.

Ultimately I am not writing to 'make the most evocative poetry possible'. I am writing to heal. I am not bothered if no one else appreciates my work, or even reads it. All I really care about is expression and the benefits gained. Thus, I will put down the words as they come, advice be damned. I encourage you to treat your work in the same way. **Learn the rules so that you know how to break them. But beyond that, just write. A pure expression of the heart will**

be infinitely more powerful than a formulaic rendition of a played-out cliché. That said, I actively study the craft so that I can better understand and express myself. Knowledge is power, and sometimes all it takes to elevate a piece of work to the next level is some small piece of guidance, or the application of a tried-and-true principle. My advice with this book is to try it all, keep what works, discard what doesn't, and add your own flair to the mix.

I choose to share my work, both here and online, but you need not feel obliged to do likewise. You are writing for yourself. For your art. For expression. For healing. That said, if you do feel so inclined or inspired, I would love to read your work, so please reach out and share it with me.

Let's get writing!

Part 1: What Is Poetry?

When words become art...

Poetry is just words on a page.

Anything beyond that definition risks falling into a philosophical or literary debate that would amount to such an abstraction of the beauty of the artform as to render it pointless. **There are no rules. No restrictions. No limits to what you can and can't, or to what you should and shouldn't do.** A lot of this book will help you to hone that expression,

14

giving you tips, tools, and tricks to make it more evocative. But that is all just make up and window dressing. Expression is the key. Some people gravitate towards rhymes and structure, others to free-flowing verse, others still, to long form paragraphs or books, crafting each line with meticulous care. It is all just writing. It is all just words on a page. It is all just poetry.

Sometimes you won't know what kind of writing is coming. Is it a poem, a podcast script, a blog, or a book? Maybe it's something else entirely, like a painting or dance. Time and practice will give you an intuitive sense of what it is and how to proceed. Consider *No Longer Able To Swim*, it could easily have been written as a short story, hitting similar beats and symbolism – but it landed as a poem.

No Longer Able To Swim

Overwhelmed
By the responsibilities
I volunteered for
Way back when
I believed

Now I see
That a life raft
Can be come a stone

All it takes
Is one hole
And everything sinks

I am no longer able to swim

Weighed down
By all the things
That were supposed
To help me
Survive

If I was instead to have applied the tools, tips, and tricks of short fiction, perhaps it would have been expressed differently, or perhaps I am just in a poetry phase. The point is that an idea can be expressed in multiple formats, multiple times, but I have found that getting it down in its purest form, at least initially, leads to the best version of expression, and from there you can play.

Consider the first few paragraphs of this section. They came to me in the above format, but with some tweaking, line breaks, and other applications of the tools from this book, perhaps a poem will form. Let's have a quick play…

just words on a page

poetry
just words on a page

anything more
is an abstraction
just a pointless debate
attempting to pin down the impossible

there are no rules
there are no restrictions
there are no requirements

beyond
just words on a page

Clearly not my best work, and I didn't spend much time on it, but that kind of proves my point. The feelings conveyed in the poem, to me at least, are better expressed in the longer format above. What's more, that is the format that I was inspired to write in, thus the full force of my care and application of creativity and technical prowess was brought to bear upon the former, but I lacked such desire for the latter. **The point is, write the words down, as they come, and then play. Perhaps you are writing a poem, perhaps not. Either way, just write.**

Broadly speaking, there are two different types of poetry: 'free form' and 'structured'. As the name suggests, free form is free, the poet is not limited to any rules, structure, or restrictions other than those they impose upon themselves. On the other hand, structured poetry has a predetermined set of rules in which the poet needs to work towards for their piece to be deemed acceptable; think of the limitations contained within the ABAB, haiku, monorhyme, sonnet, limerick, acrostic, etc. People get very finicky in the debate over these definitions, arguing endlessly about whether a certain poem meets the criteria of a particular type of poetry. To me this is all mute. I do not care if a poem fits a definition or not. I just care if it moves me (I am more artist than scholar!). **In my opinion, there is no best way to write poetry and no best type.** I encourage you to play with every variation of form that appeals to you – and even those that don't - this will help you to discover the intersection between what you enjoy writing and what you are good at writing. Practice makes perfect so work on your craft.

This book is not going to give you a guide to the specific technicities of a Shakespearian Sonnet or other traditional forms of poetry. There are far better resources available for that, see Part 6: Resources. In this book, I will not go into quatrains or how to ensure that you are following the iambic pentameter perfectly. I will not talk about the issues of translation that cause the traditional 5,7,5 syllable haiku structure to be questioned when writing in English, nor will I spend much time worrying about if a poem should be considered an ode, villanelle, or a limerick. **Instead, the focus will be on making your poetry, however you choose to write it, evocative.**

A poignant example of a freeform poem that moved both myself and my audience was *this morning i woke*. Written as a kind of narrative, this poem inspired countless comments and messages – some of concern, but vastly more sharing a resonance with the themes of Lovecraftian horror that the concept of a scary 'nothingness' evokes. This poem has no structure, and was largely written off the cuff, with only minor edits to eliminate superfluous words and to sure up some other hanging sentences.

this morning i woke

this morning i woke
terrified of nothing
my anxiety already overworking itself
working me up to a state of near panic
i tried remembering that i am safe
it didn't help
i tried breathing slowly
but i couldn't
so my body tried to vomit out the non-existent toxins
of which it believed itself afflicted
i doubled over
i fell to my to my knees

and expelled everything
and in the slight pause
between the release
and the wiping of the mess off my beard
i had moment of reflection
i began to laugh
how silly i thought
to be so afraid of nothing
how ridiculous is my anxiety!
what a joke!
looking down at last nights dinner
i felt empowered
but that empowerment was quickly quashed
a dead weight in the depths of my gut began to form
a weight so heavy that even the most adamant
of retching couldn't dislodge
the laughter ended
new thoughts replaced old
and i realised
that true nothingness
is beyond terrifying
that the opposite of fear isn't calm
the opposite of sadness isn't happiness
the opposite of hate isn't love
no
the opposite of all of those things
the opposite of everything
is a nothingness so vast
so all encompassing

that i couldn't comprehend a merest portion
awed by the paradoxical size of the nothingness
i wept
but then i laughed once more
for that weight in my gut
and the sheer terror that it evoked
told me
that for now at least
i am living on the opposite side of the nothingness
my anxiety is right
i should be afraid
but i should also
be grateful of the fact
that i can wake
terrified
vomiting
and unable
to slowly
breathe

Would *this morning i woke* have been more powerful if it were altered it to fit a specific structure? Personally, I don't think so. When choosing between writing a free form or structured poem, I generally go with the choice that will result in the most evocative poem, and I invite you to do the same.

What Is Evocative Poetry?

Good art moves people. It changes their emotional state – usually from neutral or mellow, towards any extreme. This change isn't always in the positive direction. Good horror will terrify you, a masterful comedy will have you in hysterics, and any existential thriller worth its salt will leave you questioning the very nature of reality and the people within it.

With every poem I write, I aim to move emotions; at least my own, and ideally the reader's. Else, what is the point? Why bother writing or sharing it? Why should I or anyone care? Of course, art is subjective, so not every poem will move every person in the same way, but you do know for certain when you have been moved. It's the goosebumps and corresponding sense of awe and wonder. It's a feeling of discovery, of witnessing the transformation of words on a page into something ethereal.

Like all art, poetry is subjective. **Determining what makes something 'good' is like trying to pin down mercury; very challenging and likely to drive you insane.** Nevertheless, some poems simply seem to pop. Mere words on a page magically transform into vivid, evocative imagery that moves us. It resonates with a core aspect of our soul, it opens new lines of contemplation, it shows us truths we never suspected to exist. Excitedly we show these revelatory poems to a friend, only to find ourselves stupefied by their lack of a response. For whatever reason, they didn't connect, and the poem fell flat.

Writing your own poetry adds many more layers of complexity to the mix. You find yourself wanting to aptly express your inner world, searching for the perfect blend of symbolism, rhyme, and structure, only to find yourself coming up short. Perhaps you simply cannot get the words out of your mind and onto the page, or maybe you find yourself stuck in endless loops of revision, never quite happy with the final product. Perhaps you know that you are capable of 'more' or 'better' writing but are, as of yet, unable to produce. The point is, for whatever reason, you are not happy with your poetry and want to improve. If you then choose to share your work, the self-doubt, confusion, and fear of judgement will compound those feelings and potentially stifle your creativity altogether.

This book will help.

The truth is people like what they like. Their opinion of your work is not a judgement on you as a person – rather it is a subjective view of some words on a page, consumed in the moment. Their judgement is likely a product of their mental states, upbringing, genetics, life circumstances, current tastes, desires, and friendship groups. **Notice how none of this has anything to do with you?**

I feel your fears, I hear those questions reverberating up from the depths of the darkness, silently screaming, 'What if I am judged? What if I am laughed at? What if someone thinks my work is childish, lame, or basic. What if no one reads it? Or worse still, what if everyone does?

On People Reading My Poetry

I break down my readers into three broad categories of people:

1: The 'Inner Circle'. These are people who are close to me, people who support me unconditionally, who love and encourage me, who want me to grow, and who will give me feedback that I trust. This is a very small group. Whilst it is hard to share some of my darkest truths with this group, they ultimately accept it – or at least accept my need to express it.

2: The 'Unknown Circle'. These are people I do not know in my personal life. The fans, the haters, and everyone else who has discovered my work. It can take time and practice to get comfortable sharing to the world at large. People can be extremely critical and extremely complimentary – both of which can be problematic for different reasons if taken too seriously. Consider the poem *Do You Love Me, Or Just The Idea Of Me?*

Do You Love Me, Or Just The Idea Of Me?

Do you love me,
Or just the idea of me?

I may be your 'dream girl'
But I am real,
And that reality is different
From your fantasy.

How often must we fight,
Just to clarify
That you expected
Me to speak differently?

How many tears must fall,
Just to realise
That you expected
Me to be something I'm not?

If you love me,
Please drop your expectations
And open your eyes
To the real me.

My body has blemishes.
I will lose my temper.
I judge unfairly.
I get things wrong.

I am not perfect,

No one is.
Unless of course,
They're just a dream.

On the day that I shared that poem, I received these two pieces of feedback:

Feedback 1: "I feel like I have gained a deeper understanding of the complexities of love and relationships. The author's insights into the importance of being honest with ourselves and our partners and the need for genuine connection in our relationships are both valuable and thought-provoking. This poem has given me a lot to think about and inspired me to examine my own motivations and desires when it comes to love. I would highly recommend this poem to anyone who is seeking to build stronger and more authentic relationships."

Feedback 2: "Sucks to be her then lol. Every woman is an Empress(sic) inside. Your subject is quite pitiful. Not as good look."

Ideally, I would have all my poems produce the same revelatory response in all my readers as suggested in the first feedback. Ideally, my work would be received with such reverence as to render Feedback 2 an impossibility. But we don't live in an ideal world, and as these feedbacks show, the same piece can illicit two vastly different responses.

If I were to take Feedback 1 on as truth, not only would I risk becoming an egotistical narcissist, but also my poetry could suffer. To replicate the magic, I may twist my style or only write in a certain way to illicit such a response – perhaps I would be successful, perhaps not, but ultimately I know for the sake of my own growth as a writer I need to focus on expression far more than reception. Conversely, if I were to take Feedback 2 as truth, not only would my confidence risk being shattered, but I may consider changing my writing style or topic choice to avoid such 'pitiful' topics. To avoid all of this, I follow the adage,

"You are not as good or as bad as they say, you are."

This helps me to maintain a level head regardless of what responses I am getting to my work. What's more, I make sure to check myself whenever anyone from the Unknown Circle (or anyone really) offers me feedback or advice. If I didn't ask for it, I tend to take it with a grain of salt – I talk elsewhere in this book about how to appropriately ask for and accept feedback.

3: The 'Outer Circle' is everyone else. Here is where you may come across some issues, both in relation to your expectations of them, as well as their reception to you as a poet.

Initially, I had the naive (and unfair) expectation that everyone I knew would care about and read my work. I assumed that they would all buy a copy of my book and speak positively of it to their friends, encouraging them to purchase it as well. But of course, what I am writing is not for everyone, thus most of the people I know would be excluded based on genre and medium alone. Of those who remain, many will find themselves blocked by the fact that they know me and thus cannot separate the art from the artist. Apparently this is a common feature; even best-selling authors talk about how those close to them simply cannot read their work. I learnt to lower my expectations of this group and taught myself to realise that although my latest book is extremely special to me, to them, it is just another thing that one of the many people they know are doing. In the same way I am not equally engaged in projects of everyone I know, I cannot expect everyone I know to be engaged in mine. That said, some of my work has resonated with people in the Outer Circle and has subsequently brought us closer – for this I am tremendously grateful.

Unfortunately, there is a much darker and harder to navigate part to the Outer Circle - the people I least want to read my work are those who don't have my best interests at heart. These are the people who have hurt, judged, critiqued, or belittled me, or suggested 'lovingly' that there is no future in what I'm doing here. **I know someone is in this group when I *care* that they know I am writing. These people do not make me feel safe about the prospect – not in the way a total stranger may make me feel unsafe, but rather in a 'by reading my work they will know me with a level of intimacy that I am not comfortable with' kind of way.** To invoke a physical analogy for a moment, I would prefer people from the Unknown Circle to see my nude body than anyone from this part of the Outer Circle. The former may judge me in the same way as the latter, but ultimately I do not know them, nor have a history with them, so those judgements simply do not land with the same kind of force. I just don't care anywhere near as much.

Navigating the Outer Circle is a challenge. If you are writing only for yourself, you may avoid this problem entirely, but if you ever plan on releasing your work there is a risk that any or all of the members of the Outer Circle will read your work – and take it personally. I am of course talking from experience. Sometimes, some of my work, is in fact about these people - or more specifically about my response and emotionality to them or their actions. But other than with my father, who is now deceased, I don't mention anyone by name, or title, and never will. But nonetheless, conflict has arisen, and relationships have been lost. But to be fair though, there wasn't much of a relationship anyway, so I was disappointed but okay with letting them go. Ultimately, I felt like I had to always act around them anyway, and them reading my art was like them seeing my truth for the first time – something that some simply couldn't accept.

There is no easy way to navigate the Outer Circle, other than to say it gets easier. You get used to it. You accept it and you accept yourself. Writing heals you and you grow into someone new, and you learn to love yourself despite the judgements that come explicitly or implicitly. **You learn to accept how much it hurts and simultaneously how little you care**. It is a unique process that only you can navigate. I know that were my father alive, I wouldn't find sharing my work anywhere near as easy. That said, perhaps I would have reconciled some of the pain directly with him and perhaps talked through many of the issues I am instead forced to express through poetry. I don't know which version of reality would be preferable, but I am living in this one, so I need to make do with what I have got.

I started sharing with the Inner Circle, then the Unknown Circle, and kind of just left the Outer Circle to discover my work, planning on dealing with the fall out, when and if it arises. Was that the best approach? Probably not, but it was what was necessary for me to progress as a writer, and ultimately as a person healing from trauma. Sharing my darkness and light in the form of poetry is the ultimate reclamation of my past and I am feeling more empowered each day because of it.

You could always choose to write under a pseudonym, but the truth may still come out. If you feared that possibility, you would not be writing with the same tenacity and vulnerability necessary to write truly evocative poetry. To call this a shame would be a vast understatement.

My approach is to share whatever arises, and then, if there is an issue that arises from the sharing, I write about those issues and share some more.

What Should You Write about?

Write what you know, not what you think will sell.

One of the main problems creatives of all persuasions have, is that they attempt to replicate the current trends. They see what is working and then try to do it themselves, only to get discouraged when they fail to see similar results. Some will tweak and refine and practice until they get it right, but the vast majority won't. Most of them will give up, put down the pen, and stop writing all together. This is a shame, more so for the fact that it is easily avoidable.

Your best work will come from what you know, what you have experienced, and most importantly what you need to express. That successful artist is successful because they have honed their unique expression of their artform. **They are creating like themselves, not attempting to replicate the success of another person.** I talk about voice and style and creative choices elsewhere in this book, but for the moment I just want you to focus thematically on what you know and feel. Turn the lens inward and introspect on what is desperately crying out to be expressed. Start there and get it all out. Once you have done so, you will discover that there is more depth to the infinite complexity of your inner world. Over time, your topics, theme, and delivery will become more nuanced and varied, and as it does, your art will become ever more evocative. You may never write like your favourite poet, but you will learn to write like yourself – ultimately a far more satisfying experience, both for you and your readers. **If they wanted that artist, they would read their work, not your attempt to replicate it.**

When you write what you know, you can go deep. You can express the nuance and complexity, you can embody truth, and present it on the page in a way the perfectly represents your lived experience. Over time you will begin to become known for your style and expertise in writing about it – and perhaps some people will want to replicate your style!

What If Your Readers 'Don't Get It'?

Communication, either via words on a page, or spoken, is not perfect. The speaker formulates a concept in their mind (imagery, feelings, sensations, memories, emotions) and condenses all of that down into words and expresses it. Grammar and syntax help that expression when the medium is a page, and tone and body language help that expression when the medium is spoken word. It is then the receiver's job to read (or listen) to the words and reconstruct the code back into imagery, feelings, sensations, memories, emotions, and all the other unseen, internal, mind stuff - and interoperate it all. Writing is a one-sided version of this process, and a conversation is this process repeating itself both ways.

Ever read a book that leaves you confused, or better yet observe a conversation between two other people who are clearly not understanding the other person's point of view, or are speaking through each other? This is an issue inherent to all forms of communication and relates directly to the worry of your readers 'getting' your work. The truth is, they won't get it – how can they? They don't have your lived experience. All they are getting is scribbles on a page that their brain is trying to make sense of and interpret.

If I was to say that I am sad. What am I actually saying? You have an idea, you have a broad sense, but you don't quite know exactly what I mean. This applies to all words - we are playing with the finger pointing to the moon. The finger points and says look there, there is the moon. But unfortunately, the only way to get to the moon is to go there for yourself. **We can point the way, but there is a gap that is filled by the reader's internal state.**

Three simple examples to prove my point:

1: If I was to ask five of my readers to describe the emotion of anger, what are the chances that they will come up with the same thing?

Maybe this is too abstract. What about if I was to describe, in detail, a leaf on a tree and ask them to draw it (or perhaps select the best representation of the leaf from a selection of 100 options). What are the chances that the results would be remotely similar?

2: Grammar, syntax, italics, emphasis, tone, body language and other modifiers of words all impact interpretation differently and themselves will all be interpreted differently by different people. Take the sentence, 'I didn't steal your car', seems clear enough right? But watch what happens when I italicise each word, thus emphasising it. Notice how the meaning changes each time.

I didn't steal your car.
I *didn't* steal your car.
I didn't *steal* your car.
I didn't steal *your* car.
I didn't steal your *car.*

3: Consider your reaction to the following poem, *Love Is*

Love Is

Love is a mortgage,
A debt promise of pain.
Paid with interest,
For those you outlive.

Love is making connections
Despite knowing they will be broken.
And it's the letting go
Of the guilt for doing so.

Love is for the small sacrifices,
That contain the hidden joys.
And the memory that's both
Blessing and curse.

Love is knowing when to push,
And when you must concede.
The realisation that you're wrong,
And the leaving of transgressions unseen.

Love is the give and take,
The unspoken word.
The comforts freely given,

And those gratefully accepted.

Love is the discipline to say no,
Through begging, pleading and pain.
And the careful observation,
Of limits reached.

Love is tempered guidance,
A shot at eternity.
And the words of encouragement,
To try once more.

Love is a partnership,
A bonding of the muse.
A step into darkness,
Taken together in faith.

Did that poem resonate with you, or are some aspects of it off in some way? Have I nailed it, or is it so totally off the mark as to make you question your choice of purchasing this book? Truth is, this poem has received all of these responses and more. None of them are objectively 'correct', but nevertheless each reader is subjectively correct in their interpretation. **The point is, what I write and what you read may look the same, but the internal experience will be vastly different.** As too may be my intention of each piece. Do you even know if it was my intention to describe what love actually 'is'? The title suggests as such, but when a poem is simply presented as above, the reader doesn't know what was going through the author's head, nor what they were trying to accomplish with the piece. Perhaps it was meant to be one part of a larger collection, maybe it was written as a homage to another famous poet, perhaps it was an attempt to express an ideal that is found only within media, or written as a response to a recent experience. Maybe it is an idealistic representation of something that can never be fully experienced, or was written as an accompanying piece to an essay or talk. *Love Is* could be any of those things or something else entirely – you will never know.

So no, your readers won't necessarily get your poetry in the way you intended it, but that is okay. Our goal is to move the reader emotionally. To leave a mark. To impact them. To make them want to read more of our work and to share it with their friends. We can try to evoke certain feelings, but we can never do so with 100% effectiveness or accuracy.

How To Approach Writing

Writing feels akin to a combination of exorcising a demon, giving birth, and the following of a holy calling. There is a reason you are reading this book. It is the reason you want to write. You may not even be able to articulate it, beyond a drive, a push, a

37

force, that seems to be moving you in a certain direction. You know when you hold the negative poles of two magnets, how one is compelled to move? You can hold it back, but there will forever be tension.

Back when I started, I was running. I knew what I didn't want to be, or rather I needed to pin it down on the page, effectively creating a massive warning sign that states 'danger, do not enter'. My past held demons, but I didn't yet know where to go to escape them.

The calling came next; the small still voice, gently putting me onto a path, or perhaps helping me to create it. A compass pointing to my true north, the distant mountain I am to summit.

Then came the climb, or perhaps the birth. Then, as now, with this book, it is a process of deep learning, change, challenge, and introspection. Each time I look at the summit prior to starting out, I believe I can. Then halfway through I see just how much further I must go – and question everything. But a birth can't stop halfway. It is coming whether I want it to or not. So ultimately, I find myself both pushed and pulled, by a force outside of my control, and find myself pushing and pulling with everything in my control to safely arrive at the summit, to safely birth my baby.

My first job was at McDonalds. Back then they operated on a push system, the workers would pre-emptively make a bunch of Big Macs, waiting for the customers to choose them. Then McDonalds switched to a pull system. Nothing was premade, a Big Mac would be made to order. Each approach has its positives and negatives, and whilst the pull system resulted in fresher food, it was slower. Thus, during peak times, customers had to wait longer because we could no longer cook in bulk.

I share this with you here because there is an analogy to writing. **You need to find the approach that works for you**. I used to approach all my writing as a push system. I would look for external direction, I would write to a topic or whatever current affair was in the news, or I would answer a university essay question. This 'worked' as I was able to get the job done, but it wasn't inspired. It wasn't magical. My work had little soul. But I was able to produce. Output was functional and predictable. Unfortunately, this approach doesn't work for me with poetry – it may for you though so don't discount it just yet.

I write poetry on a pull system. The universe, the muse, my creativity, the poem itself, or some other sort of force seems to demand that a poem is written. I have learnt to listen to the customers' orders so to speak, ensuring that I am ready to create when that order comes. You have probably felt this yourself. The shower thought, the idea that wakes you up at night, the concept that grasps you out of the malaise of existence and into the world beyond. Something is coming and it simply must be written.

I have learnt to both give myself the time and space to be open to receiving those orders (meditation, down time, silence), and ensuring that I always have a tool on hand and ready (notepad, phone, laptop). Every person's process, like every restaurant, will have their own unique approach to creation, and to creating different things on the menu. My poetry is pure 'pull', but my books, podcasts, blog, and fiction are a combination of both. I am pulled to an idea, but then I need to dedicate the time to push it into existence.

Treat Yourself Like A Professional

Finding the time to write can be hard and staying focused during that time can be harder still. Whether or not you are like me and want to make money off your art (gasp!), or just write for the sheer pleasure or catharsis of it, you will want to make the most of the limited time you get with the page. Above and elsewhere in this book, I talk about 'being open' to poetry coming, but here I want to talk about optimising the use of time you have carved out of an otherwise full schedule. The crux of my suggestion is to **treat the creative part of yourself as an employee** of sorts. Put yourself on the clock and ensure that you are working towards a goal that matters – not wasting time on social media or doing other busy work that isn't taking you closer towards your creative goals.

The first step is to prioritise what you want to accomplish before sitting down to a session. Yes, there are hundreds of things you could be doing, but which single one would be the best use of your time? For me, right now, its writing this book. I feel like it will be the most impactful for the world and my career at this moment. Yes, I could write more poetry, or work on a podcast, or share a social media post, or do my taxes, or whatever, but none of those things will move the needle of success as far as finishing this book will. Besides, once I have finished writing, I will pass it onto my editors (hello and thank you!) and during that time, I will work on other things.

It takes practice to determine the lead domino. You first must know what you want to accomplish in the long term and what steps it would take to get there, and then you must have the dedication and discipline to put everything else aside and work. Don't fall into the trap of 'just doing a little' of other tasks – before you know it, your time will be gone, and you won't have much to show for your efforts beyond some relatively pointless tasks being crossed off the to do list. Those will wait. Your muse won't.

The second step is to **set yourself a strong intention prior to starting**. Tell yourself what you are going to do and why it matters. I use *The Writers Creed* for this purpose; something I wrote for myself, then printed off and placed prominently upon my wall. I read it daily before I begin a session, and if it resonates, I encourage you to do the same, or even better write your own.

The Writer's Creed

I am a writer.
I have given myself this time to write.
This time is sacred.
I will not waste it.
I will not worry about the quality, worth, or potential audience.
I will just write.
I will get the words on the page, as they come, without judgement, without filter.
I will write because I love it, because I have something to say, and because writing heals me.

And when the time is up, I will let it go, until I sit down to write again.

Finally, **if all else fails, consider 'hiring yourself'** ... let me explain. Despite everything I've mentioned in this section, I used to have a tendency to waste a significant proportion of my available writing time, primarily because I wasn't taking it seriously. There was no boss hanging over my shoulder implicitly pushing me to work, and I was under the (false) illusion that all creativity was magic and had to always be a product of inspired spontaneity - there certainly is an aspect of magic, but that magic can be conjured as I expand upon elsewhere. This attitude was given a stark contrast to my attitude when working for others. If I am on the clock, I am working, and desperately want to ensure that I am accomplishing what is required, so that both the boss and the customer are happy. In a way, the fact that it isn't my business conversely made me care about it more, likely because of the implicit social pressures and societal conditioning combining with my social anxiety. This tendency of mine isn't a bad thing – it ensures that I can maintain employment and work to standard. But the discovery of the contrast was revolutionary. It made me ask myself 'Why don't I treat my own work just as, if not more seriously?'

Why don't you?

For me it was a fear of failure, a perfectionist complex, and a lack of faith that anything I was doing was 'worth it' beyond more than just a casual hobby on the side; self-worth issues are rife!

So now, I hire myself. 'Employer Zac' is a bit of a hard arse. He expects results, expects me to turn up on time, and expects me to get the work done. He watches over me and knows when I am slacking versus when I am thinking or resting. He creates a work environment, conditions, and schedules that will optimise my output and then ensures that I stick to them. He analyses what makes a day a success or a failure and makes the appropriate changes. He determines the priorities I will work on each day, but also is aware of my mental state and capabilities on a given day and adjusts his demands as such. Then, once the day's work is done, he thanks me for my time, and I am free to pursue other aspects of my life.

This reframing of my time has done wonders for my productivity and creativity. I am getting more accomplished and of a higher standard. Importantly, my creativity hasn't been killed in the process, primarily because 'Employer Zac' knows about the information within this book and encourages me to employ it if I face a block. Simply put, I want to be writing as much as I possibly can each day, but the world is loud and distracting, and sometimes my mental state isn't (initially) as focused as it could be.

This approach is ostensibly just a mental game I am playing with myself – but it is akin to 'being your own parent' and looking after your health by making adult choices around diet, alcohol, and exercise. It isn't fun to do, but doing so allows you to live your best life. Hopefully this approach will allow you to live your best writer's life - if you find yourself at the end of your allocated writing time, upset with how little you accomplished, or annoyed that you didn't work on the right tasks, or that you were distracted on social media or other trivial matters, consider this approach. What you need from your 'employer' will vary from me but having a serious person, even if it is you, looking over your shoulder from time to time will help you to stay on track – how can it not?

If you felt a bit of a pull back at the idea of hiring yourself, or establishing times in which you will be creative, or feel like you cannot train yourself to be creative, you may need to reframe exactly what you feel art and creativity in general is, and where it comes from.

There is a reason you are reading this book; it is because part of you at least believes that it is possible to get better at writing poetry. That is, **you can do certain things and your creativity will begin to unlock**. In my experience and that of my students, to write good poetry you just need the willingness to be open to it coming and the perpetration to catch it when it does.

The following things tend to help: Extended silence, time without distraction, focused attention, a dedicated intention to be creative, a lack of attachment to the outcome.

Discovering and implementing what works for you, when combined with the practicing of various techniques and approaches to creative writing, will result in your ability to write evocative poetry improving. Yes, some people will be more naturally gifted, but over time and with the right choices, you will be able to vastly supersede both their quality and quantity. It will feel like you are on some kind of performance enhancing drug for creativity, speaking of...

The Relationship Between Drugs & Creativity

There is a risk for poets, and all artists, to believe they need to be drunk or high to be creative. And whilst I have had some amazingly creative thoughts whilst stoned, rarely, if ever have, I produced anything of worth in that mental state. Obviously everyone is different, but I prefer to work with the creative energy sober, for two main reasons: health and practicality. Put simply, I want to create as much as possible, as often as possible, so **getting drunk or high all the time, isn't feasible for life**. Not only would it impact my functionality elsewhere, but the effectiveness of taking the substance would diminish to a level where I would feel more 'normal' when stoned and sobriety would be a discomforting and unproductive annoyance. This isn't practical and I have seen many talented people fall into that trap. The pattern is always the same, initially the drugs 'help' them to create, but quickly they resort to thinking about the art as opposed to creating it. Over time their mental and physical health deteriorates and their art is all but forgotten. They become the embodiment of the struggling artist in all ways, bar actually doing more than the occasional piece of art – often something so esoteric that it appeals only to them. This is because **the very nature of drugs often makes all thoughts**

and expressions, seem profound. But upon sobriety, that profundity is lost. What was so beautiful, resonate, and glorious fades by the next day and simply doesn't land. This is my experience but obviously your process, lifestyle, and creative requirements will be different. I just caution you against those feelings of 'need' when it comes to substances and art. You may *need* it to be creative, but then again, addictions have a way of justifying themselves, and sadly many artists fall for this trap.

Don't get me wrong here, I am not advocating straight edged sobriety. I have used on occasion and will do so again - but for specific reasons. I have found that contemplating large projects, creativity in general, and my ability to share my art with the world, has been significantly enhanced by (very occasionally) getting high. I feel like it shows me a potential future, opportunities for me to explore, and novel things to consider. The seed of a lot of my projects were planted whilst stoned – but it is important to note that **the nurturing of that seed was done almost totally sober**.

Introspect for a minute on what your drug of choice does for you and see if you can put things in place to replicate its effect sober. Is it the perceived focus? The clarity of thought? The expansion of the mind? The dulling of anxiety? The switching off of the internal editor?

Perhaps instead, you could meditate prior to

writing, try exercising daily, or maybe even getting some therapy. A performance coach could help or potentially a discussion with a loved one where you openly talk though your insecurities. Would you benefit from sitting your family down and discussing ways for you to establish a work environment free of distractions? **All of this takes effort, but if you manage to crack the code to your creativity, you will unlock an internal bounty so rich that you will not be able to stop the flow of poetry flooding onto the page.**

Why Poetry?

Throughout my entire schooling career, I was a left-brain thinker. Math made sense. It had a right and a wrong. It felt like the only solid base in a chaotic world, spawned by a tumultuous home life. This was combined with incompetent and out of touch teachers and terrible examples of poetry that I simply couldn't relate to. I was left feeling that at best the entire artform was beyond me, and at worst that it was a refuge for pomposity and prose, written by people who have experienced less than they would ever write.

Flash forward a few years and life was looking a little better. I had moved out, I was safe, and I had met the woman who would become my wife. She introduced me to her poetry and shock of shocks, it resonated. We talked, shared, and expressed. She taught me the true beauty of poetry, opening me up to an artform I basically never looked at, let alone produced.

During that time, I began writing to heal. First with the book, Under The Influence, Reclaiming My Childhood, followed by a plethora of other titles in a variety of different styles. Soon, the act of writing poetry became one of my core forms of self-healing and therapy. **Like the cleaning of a wound, it hurt, but it was ultimately therapeutic**. After a conversation with a friend highlighting the potential benefits for others who may resonate with my work, I eventually decided to share it with the world, and gradually the world began to care. Now not a day goes by where I don't receive a message telling me that my poetry puts words to the thoughts they couldn't quite articulate or form themselves.

I write to heal and encourage others to do the same. This book is the logical next step after that encouragement. I can get people to agree that they should write, but a lot will immediately tell me that they can't. The fact is, initially, neither could I, and sometimes I still can't, not when it really hurt. But I have learnt to keep putting pen to paper because whether I make the words go goodly, the act of writing is healing.

There is a joy in writing evocative poetry. In knowing that your words are moving people, that you are touching upon a truth, so fundamental, so core that it simply must be written, that a blank page must be sacrificed to bring forth such beauty. Nowadays I have almost completely switched to right brain thinking and identify myself as an artist above all else. **When someone asks me what I do, I reply with, 'I am a poet'.** Not only does this steer the conversation in interesting directions, but it also cements that identity into my very essence – I suggest you start doing likewise. You do not need to wait until you are living off your work, or made a single dollar, or even really shown anyone a single piece. To be a poet, all you need to be doing is writing.

The Art Of Teaching

The creative and technical advice in this book comes from the intersection between what I have found works in practice with myself and my students, combined with knowledge gained from studying the works and methodologies of great contemporary and historic poets, writers, and artists.

I am a teacher by trade, it is my job to synthesize and express the fundamental aspects of a topic I know in depth and then present it in a way that my students can understand. Like poetry, teaching is an artform, and like all artforms, all you can really do is provide guidance for the student to consider and then integrate into their own unique expressions and world view. The goal is to help the student hone their intuitive feeling for what works, through observation, data, study, appropriate feedback, and lots of practice.

Sometimes the right information lands at the right time and produces a revolution in thinking. Other times, it sits in the background waiting for the final piece of a puzzle to slot into place before it finally clicks. Of course, teaching in real time is different than through a book. Given the limitations of the medium, some of the information presented here may not feel immediately applicable, or may seem 'obvious', and perhaps it is, but nonetheless I encourage you to **consider it all, try it out, keep what works and discard what doesn't**. Remember, your goal isn't to write like me, but to use the information here to enhance your ability to write evocative poetry.

This book is my attempt to distil the magic and science of creative poetry writing into easy-to-follow rules that you can apply to your own writing, hopefully giving you the confidence to express yourself, fully, totally, and completely.

Part 2: Creative Advice
Making the magic happen…

Don't Force Meaning

Nothing is lamer than an attempt to force a narrative, political opinion, or a buzz word topic into your poetry. Unless you are passionate about it and extremely competent, the result will come across as tacky, and importantly, it won't be impactful to the reader. I care about a multitude of issues, but I only put to paper the poems that come to me naturally. I am never happy with the results of forced poetry. After a month or two away from the piece, I find myself cringing at how obviously contrived my work was. Of course, I am critical of my normal poetry, but it is not in the same way. I had a few 'forced' poems that I could have included in my books, but I cut them all as I no longer feel what I supposedly felt when writing them originally, and upon reflection I don't think I ever felt that way.

Take the poem *Sad Zac is Sad* and compare it to *Paranoid Zac is Paranoid*. When I wrote *Sad Zac is Sad* I was writing from the heart. **It came through me, and at no point did I feel like I had to force the meaning**. It tells an abridged version of real events. The emotions, thoughts, and reasonings presented are real because I have had them. Put simply, I am speaking truth. Contrast that with the process I used to create *Paranoid Zac is Paranoid* and it is clear why it is the far weaker of the two. For a moment I smelled a potential book or at least a themed series of poems following the same format as *Sad Zac is Sad*. I toyed with the idea of writing *Stressed Zac is Stressed* and a host

52

of other pieces, all with the goal of using the choice word (sad, paranoid, stressed etc) as inspiration for both the mono-rhyme style (this kind of poem is discussed later), and theme of the poem.

The problem is that even the titles themselves fail at hitting the theme. *Sad Zac is Sad* works because it is as if a child, my inner child, is writing and naming the piece. I used younger sounding words to portray meaning, even within the title itself. But this isn't the case with *Paranoid Zac is Paranoid* – someone that is paranoid probably wouldn't write a title like that. In addition, whilst I have experienced feelings of paranoia, I have not lived it – at least not to the extent to effectively write poetry about it - thus, the forced nature of the piece. Finally, from a technical perspective, there is simply less options available in the mono-rhyme structure for words that rhyme with paranoid compared to sad – this is a hard limit that no amount of creativity can easily overcome.

Ultimately, I abandoned the idea for a series or book on this theme because I realised that many of the pieces that would potentially go in the book would feel far more like *Paranoid Zac is Paranoid* than *Sad Zac is Sad*. Furthermore, I simply didn't want to write them as the process and the result would feel more like work than play. **If I didn't want to write or read them, why would anyone else?**

I am not proud of *Paranoid Zac is Paranoid*, but I share it below for the sake of example. Contrast it

53

against *Sad Zac is Sad* and decide for yourself if it feels forced or not.

Sad Zac is Sad

Sad Zac is sad
He's feeling bad
He's feeling like he's been had
That the times he was glad
And feeling rad
Were in fact just a fad

As a wee lad
Sad Zac couldn't relate to any comrade
He was bullied by Chad
Crying, he asked advice from his dad
'Just punch his face a tad'
Lesson learnt, fists make a nomad
Add one tick to the notepad
No one approaches the battle clad
No one threatens the mad

Sad Zac is sad
Remembering his dad
Remembering him before he was mad
Rereading the notepad
Reminiscing of the success had
Ruminating on his advice to play mad

And embodying it as a personality pad

Sad Zac now fears the nomad
And trains daily for a fight he's not yet had
Fear of the footpad wielding a doodad
Has grown into fear of every comrade
'Where is the rest of the advice, dad?'
'How can I avoid also going mad?'
'What can I do to stay feeling glad?'
'Who can I turn to, now that you're just a notepad?'

Sad Zac is still sad
But also a tad glad
Because putting these thoughts on this notepad
Has alleviated some of the mad
He still feels bad
But writing has healed some of his inner lad

Paranoid Zac is Paranoid

Paranoid Zac is paranoid
Unable to understand his fellow humanoid
Every look is perceived as annoyed
Every word twisted, meaning destroyed
He fears, so he avoids
He knows he's hunted, so he seeks the void
Of course he is unemployed

Who'd want the burden of a schizoid?
There's no help from the prescribed Freud
Zac knows those pills will turn him android
Just another slave to the queen arachnoid
Just another faceless polaroid
Obedience on steroid
Given cash in exchange for a brain control fungoid
Forcing him to accept the schadenfreude, of the
doomsday asteroid

A forced poem doesn't feel the same when you are writing it. Often a poem will flow from or through you and onto the page. It will feel like the synergy between inspiration and creation and will be a joy to write – not a job. If I find myself excessively straining, or researching, or consulting a dictionary or thesaurus, that is a warning sign. If I find myself pushing something that doesn't feel alive, that is another. The only caveat is that sometimes you will find that you do need to use such tools to polish or finish off the last 10-20% of a poem – this is fine and normal, but using those tools to write an entire piece won't be enjoyable to write, and even less so to read.

The majority of *I Float* came as an analogy to the feelings I was having when starting a new anti-anxiety medication. The dull malaise induced by the medication and the associated feelings of safety were contrasted against the distant knowledge that the true excitements of life were being taken from me - all whilst I was slowly losing the ability to care, or even remember what was being lost. I didn't have to force anything about this poem, it simply came. The only things that I had to look up, or edit, after the fact was the removal of some superfluous words, as well as certain terms like 'artificiality' – I knew I wanted to describe a sense of 'fakeness', but until the piece was otherwise complete, that line remained ambiguous and unfinished.

I Float

The vastness of the ocean
Has been replaced
By the safety of a kiddy pool

I float
Under a lifeguard's watchful gaze
Passively accepting
The artificiality of my confines
Only vaguely aware
Of a time
Not long ago
When I could look upon the horizon
And feel the sun upon my skin

Memories
Of riding atop the waves

Both terrified and exhilarated
By nature's limitless beauty
Have been replaced
By the scent of chlorine
Penetrating my nose
And irritating my eyes

But I don't care
I am lulled by the warmth of the water
And comforted by the knowledge
That soon
I will forget
The taste of salt
And the thrill of that first plunge
Into the depth
Of the ocean's
Infinite embrace

Interestingly, *I Float* came to me as I was trying, and failing, to force a different poem into existence. I had just woken up from an amazing dream in which I had met and interacted with a dream girl of sorts. A person that was the perfect fit for me. A cross between a guardian angel, a lover, and mythical creature, with her own unclear and possibly dangerous motives. As of yet, the poem hasn't materialised beyond the following few lines (and another 300 words of rejected attempts). The poem may yet come, but I know that if I force anymore onto the page, I will not be happy with the result.

She Comes With The Moon

I have fallen in love
With a fantasy
She comes with the moon
A dream with in a dream
More real than reality...

I could have finished this poem off in a variety of ways — repeating the 'I have fallen in love with' refrain, or perhaps contrasted her 'coming with the moon' with her leaving with the sun. I considered tweaking it into an ABAB rhyme structure or continuing the fantasy/reality rhymes. Nothing worked, at least not without feeling forced. I could have 'finished' the poem in any number of ways, but ultimately it would be doing a disservice to the original idea, to myself, and to any readers unfortunate enough to stumble across the poem. Besides, this dream girl, the subject of the poem, deserves far more than to be immortalised upon the page in such a limited and pithy way. Perhaps I will return to *She Comes With The Moon* and by the time this book is out you will be able to read it in its entirety, or perhaps not. Maybe it will end up being the seed for a piece of fiction or some other work, or maybe here is the only place it will ever be referenced. Regardless, I am okay with this. I know that more poems will come, and I accept that for whatever reason, right now at least, this poem doesn't want to be written.

Summary

The best poems you ever write will flow effortlessly through you and onto the page. This process may hurt, but it will not feel forced. Learn to accept that sometimes you will need to wait for a poem to be ready to be written.

Write What You Know & Extrapolate Emotions

If you haven't lost a loved one, it will be exceedingly hard to capture the complexities that such a loss would entail. Life is full of different emotional experiences, some of which will have happened to you. I'd advise, at least in the beginning, to focus your efforts there. This doesn't mean you have to limit your poetry to those life events, but rather to using the emotions that you have experienced to inform and colour your work. With some introspection and imagination, you can extrapolate the emotional state that may arise from a more extreme version of a situation you have lived through.

I had a traumatic childhood; my father was a drug dealer, and I was exposed to volatile addicts daily.

60

Thus, I can talk on those experiences directly, and extrapolate the feelings of fear, confusion, shame, guilt, dissociation, lack of agency, self-worth, identity, and impotent rage. I can also easily imagine how similar childhoods and traumatic experiences may feel. **But the further from my truth I get, the harder it is for me to write authentically – not without many honest discussions with other people who have lived it.**

Compare *The Derelict*, a poem about one of my father's clients, with *On The Field of Failure*, a response to war and conflict, and you will clearly see that I have had a significant amount of direct lived experience with the former, and not much with the latter. I have not seen war firsthand, I have not been displaced, and I have not experienced the fear, confusion, trauma, and dread that I imagine would come with such an experience. The only experience I can speak to is the sterile news reports and histories, chronicling what feels like another round of pointless death. My experience is of a helpless outsider saddened by what is occurring, but feeling powerless to stop it, whilst also knowing that I am safe, in my home, halfway across the globe.

This difference shows itself in the language and flow of both pieces. *The Derelict* places you vividly in the action. You are right there, seeing and feeling the emotionality that I felt. But with *On The Field of Failure*, I wanted to emphasize the feeling of pointless

61

repetition, with the entire poem having the goal of setting up the final line of 'nothing changes on the field of failure'. The repetition of the reframe contrasted against the dulled sadness of each changing sentence highlights the pointlessness of war – as seen from someone who hasn't been there and who has not lived it.

The Derelict

The first thing you notice are his bare feet,
Black and dirty.
Lacking a chair, he squats.
Lacking a home, he squats.
The second thing you notice are his eyes,
Sunken and hollow.
Desperate.
You walk.
He sees you seeing him.
You walk faster.
He smiles wide.
His teeth are as broken as the dwelling he guards.
Shattered windows for a shattered soul.
He calls out.
You walk faster still.
His sunken eyes suddenly grow sharp.
He recognises an opportunity.
You wear things of value.

You are something of value.
A second voice joins the first,
And then a third.
They point.
They chuckle.
They stand.
Your wealth represents their high.
Your body represents their high.
You run

On The Field Of Failure

Black crows gather
On the field
Of failure

Iron rusts
On the field
Of failure

Blood stains the grass
On the field
of failure

Orphans are made
On the field
Of failure

Nothing changes
On the field
Of failure

The more experienced a writer you become, the more you will be able to write on topics and speak to aspects of the human existence you haven't directly experienced – or anyone for that matter. Entire genres of fiction are predicated on this exact ability, with wildly successful authors moving countless readers, taking them on fanciful journeys into the previously unknown.

That said, the emotionality and connection the reader feels is real, and has been experienced before, time and time again. Don't mistake setting, theme, plot, content, or any other aspect of writing for the emotional connection of the reader. It is no different with poetry. You could write a poem about the lamentations of a magical spider saying goodbye to her last child before she embarks on an intergalactic journey to meet with a distant god. There is nothing stopping you. But if you wanted that poem to resonate with anyone beyond a small group of arachnophiliacs and fantasy enthusiasts, **you better ensure that the real, grounded, and human emotionality of the moment is being conveyed** – fear, excitement, trepidation, hope, awe, etc. If you don't, the reader will be lost and will not care. The good news is that you have likely felt such feelings before and can thus use your imagination to extrapolate those feelings onto a unique situation and thus produce said poem. Obviously this example is highly fanciful, but it serves a point. You can write on whatever you like, but the more you have experienced whatever is truly at its core – the emotionality – the better the end result will be.

I would like to contrast two poems, that on the surface seem to be discussing the same thing *Setraline* and *Take The Damn Pill*. These poems both focus on the topic of medication for mental health but approach them from vastly different perspectives. I wrote *Take The Damn Pill* as a response to multiple people in my life significantly struggling with mental health concerns. They were given medication which, from my perspective, seemed to be working. Yet for some reason unfathomable to me at the time, they stopped taking it and were predictably suffering with their same old problems. On the other hand, *Setraline* was written from the perspective of someone on the medication – sharing an insider view of the real impacts of taking it upon my mental state.

Take The Damn Pill

Take the damn pill,
You're on it for a reason.
It's to stop you feeling ill,
To keep you from self-treason.

Sure, you're feeling fine,
But how long will it last?
You know you're not divine,
Just look back at your past.

There was that time you went cold turkey,
When you knew it would be fine.
Instead, your mind went murky,
And you turned to a life of crime.

Or when you got the jitters,
So bad you couldn't sleep.
Feeling your skin crawling with critters,
Causing you to weep.

Or that time you almost died,
When depression came back strong.
Or the time that you lied,
To yourself that something wasn't wrong.

Take the damn pill,
You're on it for a reason.
I don't want to be reading your will,
As the last act of the season.

Sertraline

Medication?
More like calcification.

The myopic solution;
Replacing anxiety
With apathy.

Losing focus,
Focusing
On what I have lost.

My thoughts,
Circle the drain.
Both hope and fear
Falling in turn.

I am lost.

A rudderless raft,
Left to drift
Upon a dead calm lake.

Fog obscures the bank.
Fog obscures desire.

I am far too calm
To stay safe.
Life and death
Seem equally desirable.

I drift.

Cold rationality;
The last remaining
Life preserver.

The small subtle voice
Whispering
That this too shall pass;
The sun will shine,
The wind will blow,
And I will have purpose once more.

Two poems on the same topic, yet vastly different in execution and emotionality. I couldn't have written *Setraline* had I have not experienced it directly, nor could I have written *Take The Dam Pill* were I not to have lived that side of the coin either. But having done so I could, with some reading and application of imagination, probably speak to the impacts of any number of interventions, medications, addictions, and illnesses.

Finally, consider using symbolism that you know well over those you don't. In *Setraline* I reference fog, water, drains, sun, and other things I have experienced. I am sure that there are many different things that I could have substituted here, that contextually would have evoked the same meaning, but since I wouldn't have been as familiar with them, I wouldn't have used them appropriately, and thus the quality of the poem would have fallen.

Summary

All topics are available to you, but ideally you should stick with symbolism and visuals you know well and extrapolate the emotionality you have actually felt to suit the piece of poetry you are writing. Time and practice will allow you to effectively expand the scope of your poetry.

Write, Then Edit

Good writing involves two versions of yourself working on the one piece of work: Artist-You and Editor-You. These two versions of you, must work alone as **it is almost impossible to write and edit at the same time.**

Firstly, Artist-You gets into the zone, isolates themselves from the world, drinks copious amounts of coffee, does a five-minute headstand, prays to the gods, then does the myriad of other things they feel is necessary for them to get the words going goodly. They write until spent, then they put the piece aside and write something else.

At some later stage, Editor-You comes along and fixes the mess that was left to them. They tweak,

69

they change, they cut, and they correct. Editor-You can do this work because they didn't write the piece they are working on. They are detached and thus can see it for what it is and make the changes necessary to in order for it pop. Perhaps they also employ the services of an external person to assist them further.

If you are thinking about the end product whilst writing the first words, chances are you will never make it to the end anyway. A better approach, one that will get many more words on the page, is to free write. Write without worrying about what it will become, or worrying about spelling, grammar, or formatting. If you are unsure, perhaps **bold** some notes to remind yourself to return to add or tweak the gap. Or use square brackets as place holders for important details that you can't figure out yet, eg: [rhyming word here], that way you can keep writing now, and later easily search your document for what needs fixing. If you write on paper, perhaps a system of post-it notes, or a highlighter would work with a similar functionality. What matters is that you get the words out as they come and polish the piece later, when you have some time and detachment from the emotionality of the initial writing session.

I wrote *A Sun Shower* during, you guessed it, a sun shower. I was caught by surprise at the sudden change of weather, as well as the deep feelings of joy that simultaneously arose with the contrast of the sun and rain on my face. What is presented below is the

70

refined version of the poem. I wrote it during and just after the sun shower, chronicling what was occurring. The original piece was much longer, with many more superfluous words and lines that repeated the same meaning, adding nothing to the piece. Later that week, in editing, I cut them. I also tweaked the piece to include the threefold repetition of *'a moment...'* as it seemed to aptly emphasise the transient nature of the sun shower, and as I will go into in a later section, it just sounds good.

A Sun Shower

A sun shower
Beautiful nourishing chaos
Raindrops of gold
Rainbows painting clouds
Warmth of the light
Meets
Chill of the water
A moment of bliss
A moment of peace
A moment of reflection
Birds call
Wind blows
The moment has passed

We Two, Together came in a burst of inspiration.

As you will see, it deviates from my normal style (or at least it feels like it to me). For some reason, I felt compelled to lean heavily on symbolism and imagery of nature. As I was writing, another part of me was simultaneously reeling. That part, the inner critic, the editor, was telling me to stop. It was warning me that this piece would turn out clichéd and contrived. That it wouldn't be 'good' and that no one would like it. Worse still, it told me that people would judge me for not only daring to put such drivel onto the page, but for believing it worth sharing.

I try to follow my advice. Write, then edit. So, I gritted my teeth, acknowledged those parts of me providing warning, and continued to write. What is the worst that could happen? I finish it and decide it isn't that good? No harm done. It would only be me who would see my shame. Not that there is ever any shame when it comes to writing, despite how it may feel at the time. The piece that followed required some tweaking after completion, first by myself, then by my editor, who wisely recommended the removal of one line.

We Two, Together

We won't
Have much time
Together

72

But in that brief moment
Of connection
I will gaze upon you
With such intensity
As to drink up oceans
My lust
Will smother the sun
My desire
Shake the earth
I will give you my everything
Simultaneously taking
All
Of you
A fair exchange
Of passion
And pleasure
Mirrors, to one another's soul
Journals, of one another's heart
Clothing, for one another's bodies
We two
Together
In this moment
Will become
One
In every conceivable way

Originally I had the poem reading:

'A fair exchange

Of passion
Perversion
And pleasure'

My editor suggested that I remove the word perversion. I agreed, immediately recognising that the energy of that word doesn't at all fit with the rest of the poem. So why was it there first place? Well, most of the poetry I write is introspective, brooding, an expression of my inner world, or feeling about the world at large. But I also write erotica, both poetry and fiction. I thought whilst writing, that this piece would fit into that space, but upon completion, it didn't. The word 'perversion' was a remnant of that mind state and thus to make the poem more complete it needed to be removed.

Time away from a piece and the assistance of an editor can significantly improve your work.

I cannot stress enough how important it is to separate Writer-You from Editor-You, invariably if you are trying to write with the editing in mind, you will be stifled. If you are worried about what people will think, or how it will end up, or any number of other non-writing thoughts, your poetry will suffer.

Creativity is like a river - it will flow best when it is unimpeded by rocks, dams, and other debris. Some obstruction is unavoidable and fine, but too much can cause catastrophe. Your job, at least initially, is to do everything in your power to get out of your own way. To silence the inner critic (or at least let that part of you know that it will get a chance to speak later), and simply write.

In *Those Few Words* I attempt to capture a lifetime of feeling an undercurrent of disdain and judgement emanating from a certain person in my life. It took thousands of words and countless iterations to settle on the poem you will read below. The entire time my inner critic was screaming at me to stop. Telling me that I would be judged. That these poems would get back to that person and that they would cause more unnecessary drama in my life. **But instead of stopping, I acknowledged the warnings of those voices and returned to my writing.** A lot of words flowed from me that day, and I received a lot of healing because of it. I won't ever share half of what I initially wrote, because those warnings were right – it would be offensive and inconsiderate to share. But because I persisted, I was able to finally get to, and share *Those Few Words*.

Those Few Words

Those few words
Gave voice
To the silence
I always knew
Was there

Summary

When writing, just write. Put aside all thoughts of editing, reader opinion, or even the overall 'point' of the piece. Just get the words on the page and deal with the greater implications of doing so later on.

Ignore Feedback - Good & Bad

I write for myself and while I care what my readers think of my work and want them all to love it, I have learnt to ignore all feedback that I didn't ask for directly. This is an act of self-preservation. In the past, I have completely altered projects, or worse still, discontinued or destroyed them, based on unasked for feedback. Most of the time it was unintentional - they just wanted to help, believing that their insights will provide me with a valuable insight into how my writing is being perceived. The thing is, they may even be right in their perceptions, and it probably would benefit me to hear it. But unfortunately, I have somewhat of a fragile ego, and until complete, my artwork is like a delicate flower struggling to survive – if it is exposed to the elements too soon, it will fail to thrive, but if it is allowed the time and space to grow roots, it may very well thrive.

Don't get me wrong, 'Editor-Zac' loves it, but 'Writer-Zac' is crippled by it. Even the good feedback corrupts the purity of my process, because it makes me want to do more of what is loved, not necessarily more of what I want to be writing. The resulting work is never as good as the original and is always discarded. Time wasted. Lesson learnt.

Feedback comes in many forms. Take the poems *Life To Avoid* and *Spider*, the first received 25 times more likes, comments, direct messages, and shares, than the latter. These numbers suggest that I should write and share more of the first and less of the second. The problem is that I simply could not do so without coming across as forced. Also, I don't actually know what it was about the first poem that was so significantly more appreciated than the second. Was it the topic? The structure? The themes? Was it the time of day that I posted it? The accompanying picture? Perhaps it was none of these things, and I was just blessed by the algorithm Gods that day. Point is, I would be hard pressed to both know and then use that information to my advantage. I got something from writing and sharing both of those poems and wouldn't want to block off more like *Spider* in my attempts at writing another *Life To Avoid* – Besides, next time, the numbers may be reversed.

Life To Avoid

Coffee to wake

Instagram to connect
Porn to cum
Alcohol to relax
Weed to create
Coke to play
MDMA to love
News to inform
Sugar to distract
Mushrooms to pray
Valium to calm
Melatonin to sleep

Life to avoid

spider

i killed
instinctively
moving before thought
its body crushed under my heel
only in death
did I see
the beauty
of its life

A few years ago I was writing a fantasy novel. I was 20,000 words deep and they just kept coming – a writer's dream. Then, foolishly, I showed my progress to a friend who promptly offered me 'helpful' advice;

namely that there wasn't enough inner conflict in the main character to sustain the momentum of the plot. My friend was right in their feedback, the characterisation was weak. Unfortunately, their feedback shone a massive spotlight on the problem and all progress came to a grinding halt. Editor Zac was put squarely in the director seat and Writer Zac was kicked to curb and rendered effectively homeless. This resulted in me attempting to fix the problems before they were fully formed. I went back over the completed chapters, twisting and tweaking them, hoping to add that all too desirable 'inner conflict'. Suffice to say, I failed, and that book still sits in my drawer at 20,000 words, waiting for Writer Zac to return to it to have another crack.

I share this story with you to provide a solid example of when and where to ask for and hear feedback. I take full responsibility for this; my friend was just being kind. That said, if I had my time over, I would never have shown my friend the unfinished book, and if I did, I would have stopped them the moment they started giving advice. **That advice, whilst correct, was given way too early in the creative process, and thus, rather than invigorating my work, it effectively killed it.** Kind of like giving fertiliser to a plant. Too much given too soon and your tomato plant will die off – but if you wait until the appropriate time, you will find yourself with an abundance of Earth's bounty. This is as true for poetry as it is for fiction.

My practice now is to wait until I am ready, and then to ask a few trusted people for their honest opinions and then actively listen and dig deep into their responses. I want to know why they feel the way they feel – both good and bad. **It's not enough to know that they are moved, I want to know why**. I do my best to ignore any unasked-for advice. Once I share my completed work with the world, I do love receiving feedback. I read all the comments, responses, and the reviews. But I let 'Editor-Zac' do that job, because hopefully 'Writer-Zac' is too lost in the next creative process to hear what is being said about his work. And if he does, I recall the following saying, repeating it as a mantra, until the words flow once more:

"You are neither as good nor as bad as they say you are."

You may well be different to me. You may vibe off feedback like its oxygen to the fire of your creative furnace. If so, ignore all of that and do what works for you. But, if you feel like you need some space between the creative process and the response to your work, make sure you have systems in place to get it.

Finally, I want to suggest that sometimes your poems will land with some audiences and completely miss with others. Take *The Heart* as an example, on the one hand, it is silly to compare the strengths of two physical organs, but when we step into the realm of metaphor, suddenly it's not. This poem plays upon the constant interplay we all face between the mind and the heart – often two opposing forces. I wanted to leave the audience with a sense of internal passion winning out over cold logic – and for those who took the piece that way, it worked. Others however were not impressed and voiced said displeasure to me. The thing is, both opinions (and all those unexpressed) are valid. It is my job to craft the poems as best I see fit, then to share them with the world, doing my best not to take what comes back personally.

The Heart

The heart beats
Of its own accord.

Yet the mind
Can, for a moment at least,
Be pinned down in thought.

How then
Can we not say
That the heart
Is stronger than the mind?

Summary

Only take on feedback from people you trust, and only when you have asked them to give it.

Be Open To Poems Coming At Any Time

Poems have a way of just appearing. Often they come unannounced, bursting out of the silence, screaming to be heard and written down then and there. They are brutal. They don't negotiate. And they rarely give a second chance. Thus, I have learnt too always be open and ready. **I always have something to write on with me;** I sleep with a notepad under my pillow, and exercise with another close at hand. I have had the conversation with my family, letting them know that there will be times when I simply must stop whatever it is I am doing to go and write.

This isn't the case with my longer form writing – for that I need long periods of time to myself, silence, and the internal permission to allow myself to embrace the suck. That kind of writing takes work, whereas writing poetry is more akin to the capturing of fleeting inspiration. Blink and you miss it kind of deal. Take this book for instance. Writing the introduction, body, and conclusion took time and effort. Over the period of a few months, whenever I had a couple of hours to myself, I would chip away and get it done.

Interruptions were an annoyance, but nothing I couldn't address in the next writing session. The poems within the book however all appeared to me. I couldn't have completed them if I didn't write them down as they came. That said, once they were about 90% complete, their essence was captured, and I could safely let 'Editor-Zac' finish the job. Once again, your process may be different to me, and if so, lean into what works for you. But still, **be open to poems coming, and importantly, be prepared!**

Very occasionally I know that a poem will come ahead of time. It is like I can sense that it wants to be written but isn't yet ready. This was the case with *A Simulacrum of Thought*. Every morning, for months, I would watch the morning sunrise. Observing the sun against the clouds. At times marvelling at how similar, but nonetheless unique each skyline was. I knew I wanted to write about it, but never found the right way to begin. I tried forcing it a bunch of times, but as discussed elsewhere, this method produced mediocre results that I ultimately discarded. Thus, I waited, open and available, until the day it popped into my mind. I didn't predict the bleakness of the question at the end of the poem, but it seemed to fit. I was meditating on how fleeting life is, and how each day with my kids will never occur again.

A Simulacrum of Thought

Every morning
I rise with the sun
Watching with awe
The soft vibrancy
Of cloud and colour

Each sunrise uniquely its own
Yet so similar
That it's subtlety
Is often lost

A simulacrum of thought
Overlayed upon reality
Obscuring the beauty
Of the moment

How much of life
Have I lost
In this way?

Creativity, relaxation, and silence are deeply interconnected. The quieter my life is, the calmer I am, the less inputs I have, the more access I have to poetry. Every morning I meditate for 20 minutes, I get my coffee, sit outside, and simply observe the contents of my consciousness. Almost without exception, at the 15-minute mark, I am inspired. One or more poems come, and I find myself writing for another 30 minutes. This is where and when most of my work comes from. But if, before I sit down to meditate, I decide to scroll social media, or listen to a podcast, watch a video, or consume other input, my productivity is dramatically reduced. Not only do I feel less calm, but I also feel less 'connected' to whatever place my creativity comes from.

I am coming to realise just how important silence really is. We have endless opportunities for distraction – with technology the way it is, we can technically be receiving inputs from the moment of waking until the moment of sleep. This isn't 'normal' when viewed from an evolutionary sense. Until modern times, most of a person's time would have been spent in relative silence. That is something we are now missing – unless we choose to embrace it. I find that I still have an impulse to fill the silence with noise. Justifying it to myself that I am 'promoting my work' or 'learning something helpful', but when I take an honest look at why, I discover that I am just running in fear. **The silence can hold demons, it can hold pain, it can hold challenging truths I'd rather avoid – but embracing it leads to healing, clarity, and importantly to calm.**

I now only engage in an input if 'it can improve upon the silence' – most of the time it cannot. This has all resulted in an inner state that is far more fertile to creative expression. In my books 'Reflections of the Self: The Poetry, Insights, and Wisdom of Silence' and 'Mindfulness: A Guidebook

85

To the Present Moment', I talk extensively on how to integrate silence into your life, and receive the fruits of an ongoing practice of inquiry, I encouraged you to check out those resources, or more poignantly, simply to set a timer for 10 to 20 minutes and sit in silence – just remember to keep a notepad at hand!

When I say be open to poetry coming at any time, I mean it. *Connection* and *Shadow* came in quick succession during a panic attack. My partner was comforting me, calming me down, and reassuring me during the terrifying experience, when suddenly I was inspired to write. Using the voice feature on my phone I managed to dictate into the notes section, and then later when I was calmer, edit them into the format you see below. It isn't at all surprising that such an emotionally charged state would contain the seeds of poetry. A lot of my work as come from deep levels of introspection, a fall into silence, a response to a breakdown of my mental state, or as an offshoot of a dream. This is why I always keep something on me, ready to write, just in case.

Connection

A hand on my heart
You head touching mine
A word softly spoken
Connecting to the divine

Shadow

Only now
That I have stepped into the light
Do I realise
I've been living
In shadow

Summary

Be ready for creativity to strike at any time -
carry a notepad and pen, or your preferred writing
device. Foster silence to encourage further creativity.

<u>Get Inspired!</u>

If you want to write good poetry, you need to
read more than just good poetry. Don't get me wrong,
it pays to analyse and enjoy the greats. But don't limit
your options for inspiration. Read some 'bad' poetry
and question why you don't like it. Ask yourself how
you   would   convey   the   same
meaning/symbolism/feeling as the piece in a better
way. Hell, take another look at the poems in this book
and improve upon my work. Express what you think I
am trying to express in a more concise manner, one
that is unique to you. But don't stop there. Read

fiction of all kinds. Read autobiographies. Read viral Tweets. Listen to music of all genres and podcasts interviewing a variety of unique people. Watch movies, animes, documentaries, and advertisements. Got to a gallery and a sculpture park. Sit in nature and embrace unfiltered reality. Sit in silence and observe your thoughts. **The more variety of your inputs, the more tools you will have to draw inspiration from when it comes time to write.**

Similarly, **be open to expressing yourself in different ways**. You may be a poet, but perhaps you want to play with paints, or dance, or music, or some other form of self-expression. Perhaps that poem feels forced, not because you are 'a bad writer' but because that poem is in fact a painting that is desperate to be expressed as such. Who knows, perhaps after you are done painting, the words will form, and the poem will naturally come. Or not. Either way, be open and try other forms of expression as a supplement to your writing.

Mojito the Bandito came just following a viewing of 'Rango' a trippy animated kid's comedy-western. That night I dreamt of the movie and awoke to the poem almost fully formed in my mind. I wrote it down the moment I woke and then came back to it later for editing. This poem is not my usual style or theme, but it does serve as an example of the impact of different forms of inspiration aiding creativity.

Mojito The Bandito

Mojito the Bandito,
On the run from the law.
Hired an impersonator,
So in two places, he can be saw.

Committing crimes,
But seen with an alibi.
The adventures he had,
His schemes weren't shy.

The cartels took notice,
Alas it couldn't last,
Told Mojito to stop,
Or his head they would blast.

But Mojito wasn't stupid,
He had a plan to enact,
Told his impersonator to wait,
Then it was Mojito's time to act.

He shot the man himself,
Displayed his body on the town's wall.
Made the cartels happy,
And Mojito attended his own funeral.

Now he rides free,
A gun at his side.

Named Mojito no more,
His face he must hide.

Beware the masked bandit,
The criminal with no name,
He will kill you where you stand,
And leave with no shame.

The poem *Complement The Future* was inspired
by a viral photo series in which a photographer took a
picture of their subject. They then complemented the
subjects, telling them they are beautiful and took a
second picture. Many of the resulting photos are
contrasted against one another, revealing just how
impactful a complement can be.

I wanted to capture not only that feeling, but
also the foresight of the photographer in implementing
this approach and creating this set of pictures. The
photographer effectively delved into the future, chose
their words, and brought that perception of the future
to life. Now, to be clear, I have no idea what the
photographer was actually thinking or intending – but
ultimately that doesn't matter. Their work moved me
and inspired this poem, and for that I am grateful. The
point is, be open to inspiration coming from
everywhere and at any time.

Complimenting The Future

By complementing the future
she crafted the present.
Her words revealing a truth
others couldn't yet see.
Not for lack of trying,
but because she hadn't yet spoken.
The truth was merely a dream,
waiting for her to birth it into reality.
Now here, its eternal nature is manifest.
The future, now present, informs the past,
and thus her words were true before she ever spoke
them.

     The initial spark for *A Devil Resides* came in the form of an image I saw online, that had the caption 'A devil resides just under the skin'. That line triggered a string of memories of books and movies that involve a character teetering between choosing what is right and choosing what their inner devil wants. From there, it was a matter of introspecting upon my own life and discovering those movements in which I was tempted towards selfishness. Finally, the decision to turn this into an ABAB rhyme structure came from the easy follow up second line ending with 'sin', which also solidified the theme of the piece.

A Devil Resides

A devil resides
Just under my skin
Forcing upon me
Words of sin
Thoughts so close
They seem to come from within
Making me question
If I am him

Screamed threats
Of pain and chagrin
Whispered promises
Of how I can win
All I need do is
Let him in
Let him take over
And let him begin

I feel so alone
In my original sin
The darkest calling
Coming from deep within
Is there any wonder why
I run to gin?
It seems better to drown
Then to turn on kin

I've hurt people before
And my apologies run thin

But would you prefer hear them
From a jail or an inn?
Nightly I dream
Of an alternate twin
Me without a curse
Just love and a grin

Recently, I have taken to actively question and introspect upon the traditions and norms of our society. *Rose* came to me via one such session during the lead up to Valentines Day. I saw an ad that featured a bouquet of flowers and it inspired a question, 'why do we give something that is dying?'. This led me down a rabbit hole of thought that ultimately resulted in a poem.

Rose

The moment
A flower is given
It's dying

It's beauty
Wilting

It's colour
Fading

It's scent
Dulling

So why then
Do we associate
A rose
With romance?

Perhaps
The transience
Is
The point

'I love you
As you are
In this moment
And when this flower
Inevitably atrophies
I will gift you another
And another again
So you will know
That in that moment
And in every moment
I love you
Always'

Summary
Inspiration is like pouring concrete to create a
path. You need to ensure that you have enough raw

ingredients - music, movies, information, nature, conversations, etc - to complete the job. But you also need allow the concrete to set - silence and time - before it can be walked upon.

Don't Push For A Voice, Style, Or Sound

There is a concept in writers circles known as 'voice'. This is an almost ethereal, hard to pin down sound that established writers seem to have. Pick a random paragraph from one of the greats and you can just tell that they wrote it without ever knowing it was from them. Perhaps their poetry all has as similar feel, or maybe their pieces have a consistent style. You know how each song from your favourite musician is unique but somehow still sounds like them in a way that you cannot quite explain, yet you nonetheless know when another artist is desperately trying, and failing, to emulate it?

That's voice.

Truth be told, I don't see the value in trying to twist your writing into something beyond itself just to appeal to some obscure notion that seems to cripple new writers into believing that since they don't have a defined voice, they are not true writers. The reason you don't think you have a voice is because you are too close to yourself. You don't have the detachment needed to see your body of work and view it as a whole. You cannot see the aspects of your personality leaking onto the page, in ways you cannot even comprehend it doing so.

Do I have a writer's voice? Some of my readers think so and have told me as such. Ultimately, I am not concerned. I just write and I share. Then I leave it up to my readers to form an opinion. I would go insane attempting to tweak all my poetry to fit some contrived version of myself that I wanted to project. I don't have the skill needed to manipulate pure expression to both maintain the emotional impact, as well as successfully alter my cadence, word choice, and make the countless other minor tweaks necessary to construct a 'voice'.

Voice will come as it comes. The best thing you can do to assist this process is to stop thinking about it and simply write another piece. Eventually, maybe, you will be able to see your voice, or more likely, your readers will compliment your voice whilst lamenting the fact that they cannot seem to find theirs. When this happens, you can say to them, what I am saying to you now.

Just write.

Take whatever actions, internal or external needed to get out of your own way and just write.

No time? No skill? No inspiration? No space? No focus? No readers? No sales? No motivation? No support? No confidence?

Just write.

The truth is that the lights are never all green. There will always be a reason not to. There is always something 'more important' to do. Always something or someone there, preventing you from writing. Nothing I can say will remove every barrier you have, but what I can say is that everyone has barriers, and if they can overcome them, so can you. With pain. With perseverance. With effort. It won't be easy, but the struggle will ultimately be a good thing. The growth needed to overcome your unique problems will be lifechanging, and of course, you can use your suffering as inspiration for your art.

Just write.

In *Just A Fiction* and *Forever Forced To Sing* I use the same phrase 'silent screaming', with both poems addressing similar themes and feelings. It is more than okay to use the same phrases, meanings, and symbolisms across multiple poems. They are just words on a page after all, using them multiple times doesn't detract from their impact – particularly when you consider that the poems that use these similar components are unlikely to be read side by side and compared, and even if they are, so what? Just write what comes, without thought, even for your other work. Your current poem will thank you.

Just A Fiction

My entire sense of self
Is supplanted
By that one undefinable feeling
Of a nothingness with substance

A heavy emptiness
Filled
With a choking void

The screaming silence
Of a statue
Suffocating under glass

Even in the moment
When his hand
Struck my face
It didn't feel real

Even in the moment
When she exposed herself
And approached me
It didn't feel real

Nothing has ever felt real
Except the feeling of unreality

My entire life
Feels like a play
Just words in a book

Only real
When it's read
And then quickly forgotten
The trauma downplayed
Because we both know
It's just a fiction
Created for your entertainment

Forever Cursed To Sing

Can't you hear
My silent screams?
Can't you see
The rope's sway?

My head is too heavy
To cradle in your arms
I'm loathe
To drive you away

The bridges we
Walked hand in hand
You returned in secret
To burn

Thus my fate
Is bound to yours
Now the mirror's eye

Has learnt to yearn

I was blinded
By the shine
Of your porcelain
Handshake

Fooled into believing
That nothing
Would ever
Cause us to break

The memory
Of our time apart
Like the returning
Of a playground swing

Pushing against
Fate itself
Forever cursed
To sing

Oh how
I've learnt
To hold onto
All those toxic tears

Created and then
Faced together

You and I
Embodying each other's fears

The embers of
Last night's fire
Lie discarded
In their pit

Smouldering
As we dance around
No chairs left
On which to sit

I wrote those two poems years apart, but I like them both. They have a similar feel, and address similar things, but they are unique and individually powerful. None of that was intentional.

The truth is that you may never know what your voice is. You are too close to it to see it. Other people may comment that you use certain phrases, symbolisms, or styles, and that is okay – in fact, it is what attracts people to our art in the first place. You just want to avoid forcing a voice, because unless you are a master of the craft, it will be obvious and derivative, and therefore unappealing to anyone other than yourself.

Summary
Don't try to write with a certain voice, just

write, and over time it will come.

Restrictions Boost Creativity

I don't often adhere to the traditional poetic rules and structures. I prefer to write what comes as it comes. However, there is something to be said about writing with restrictions. Restrictions, be they self-imposed, or derived because of the kind of poetry that you are writing, can boost creativity. I think that one of the largest factors causing 'writers block' is having too much choice. When faced with a blank page and no prompts or guidance, most newer writers stumble and become overwhelmed. But when they are told to write a haiku on the topic of a cloudy sunrise, suddenly they get some inspiration – the result may or may not be 'good' but something is infinitely better than nothing.

I like to add my own restrictions. As a poem is forming, I start to discover what kind of poem it is. Perhaps it has an ABAB rhyme structure, or maybe it's a monorhyme, or perhaps it wants to have a certain number or lines, or specific symbolism, or perhaps each line needs to have an alliteration, or begin with a certain letter or sound. **These restrictions, even though they are self-imposed, help the rest of the poem to form.** The restrictions guide 'Writer-Zac' to keep the words coming and later enable 'Editor-Zac' to correct and tweak the wording and structure after the fact.

Once the poem is almost complete, I always consider breaking the self-imposed restrictions. I ask myself the question, 'could this poem be better if?' - I will always preference expression and readability over strict adherence to structure and restriction.

In Your Absence comes from the epic mono-rhyming poem *Can't Quite Express* – the format dictates that the ending word of each line has the same rhyme sound. I wanted to discuss the loss of a friend and all the emotionality that such a loss held. Given the length of the overall project, I didn't restrict this section's length. The restriction of end rhyme, and the topic, enabled the words to flow. That said, I didn't strictly adhere to the mono-rhyme - preferencing flow and meaning. Half rhymes and line breaks are used to emphasize certain points that I couldn't have otherwise accomplished.

In Your Absence

I can't quite express
The confusion and the mess
That's been left
In your absence
Why didn't you confess
The demons that had you possessed?

Why couldn't you
Escape the thoughts that had you depressed?
Why was this the only way you could address
The aspects of life that you detest
that had you dispossessed?
Perhaps if you got some of it off your chest
The world wouldn't be one man less
One man that blessed it with his presence
Now all who knew you are left to digest
News of the death's caress via a self-inflicted process
We can't protest
We can only attest
To the pain and existential unrest
Of the hole your life has left

In *Would You* I start each line with the words 'would you'. This restriction forces the poem to become a series of questions. With these restrictions, I tell a story by first asking the reader a series of questions, and then flip it on its head with the last question, asking them if, given the contemplation that the prior questions evoked, they would forgive me (ostensibly for acting as they themselves had).

Would You?

Would you forsake
A lifetime

Of love
For a moment
Of perfection?

Would you forestall
Happiness
For a promise
A hope
And a shared dream?

Would you forgo
A chance
To feel
More alive
Than you've ever thought possible?

Would you forgive
Me
For trying
To be more
Than I was destined
To be?

Finally, *Maya* is a haiku, and thus it is very strict on the formatting of each line. That said, the topic of 'traditional' haikus is nature, so my choice to use this structure to discuss mindfulness meditation both follows and breaks with restriction.

Maya

Silence is broken
Thoughts diverting my focus
Maya wins again

Summary
Boost your creativity by setting a restriction upon the type of poem you are going to write. This could be in the form of a traditional structure, or one that is entirely of your choosing.

Tell A Story

Your poetry can be anything you like. Yes there are technical ways to write traditional poetry, but ultimately the most evocative poetry comes from pure expression. You can use the poetic space to express a thought, a feeling, or a confusing complex bundle of emotions. You could also use it to tell a story. In addition to poetry, I also enjoy writing fiction. Sometimes I have an idea that I think would make a great short story, but I simply cannot make it happen. All my attempts feel forced, and the result isn't appealing to me or my readers. Often when this occurs, it is because I have chosen the wrong medium to express the idea. That idea may be better suited for a novel, a blog post, podcast episode, or poem.

There is no reason why you cannot tell a compelling 'short story' in the format of a poem, just make sure to include the appropriate component parts; setting, plot, character, dialogue, description, scene, etc. I tell a story with *God Asked* and *Back To Scrolling*. In these instances, telling a story helped me to express myself better than writing a poem in a different format, and the result hits harder. The reader is taken on a journey and comes out the other end changed as a result.

God Asked

God asked the man,
Why did you choose to die?
I saw no point in existence,
I couldn't fathom a reason why.

I couldn't stay focused,
I couldn't hold down work.
I'd just wait for the day to end,
to sleep away the murk.

Every day was the same,
I'd already lived it through.
What was the point of repeating
when there wasn't anything new?

What about the small changes,
the gems of love and life?
What about the lessons learnt
from surviving hardships and strife?

True, I did feel most alive
when things were at their worst.
But how is that a reason to live,
just hoping to be cursed?

I could handle the drama
but not the monotony,
nor the vagueness of existence,
nor humanity's cacophony.

I would sit alone,
I would sit in the dark,
I would sit and listen and
my mind would remark.

Highlighting my failures,
reminding me of lost dreams.
Showing me bad outcomes
and my own devilish schemes.

Where were you God,
when I needed you the most?
Why'd you only start talking

now that I am a ghost?

I was talking the whole time.
I was in the warmth of the sun,
I was in your kid's smiles,
their laughter and fun.

I was the crash of the waves,
the vision of the moon,
the spring flower's scent,
the young lover's boon.

I was the quenching of thirst,
the purr of a kitten,
the pillow at night,
the book well written.

I could go on
but I think you now know,
I was with you always,
even when you were low.

Ah God, you don't get it,
your words were too easy to miss.
What with all the noise,
with our collective descent into the abyss.

How could I just stop and look?
How could I listen to the bird's song?

How could I take a breath,
When everything was going wrong?

It isn't my place to save you,
nor can I fix your life.
I can only remind you,
that there is something beyond the strife.

That even in the midst of suffering
there are small joys to behold.
But you are right my child,
perhaps I should have been more bold.

No God, I was also wrong.
You know this was my last thought,
I could fix every problem but this one.
Oh how my family will be distraught.

God thought for a moment,
then asked the man,
If I sent you back to Earth
would you change your plan?

I will do my best,
but I make no guarantee.
I will attempt to listen,
I will attempt to see.

If *God Asked* had been a short story, I would

110

have had to spend far more time setting up the scene, crafting a way for the man and God to be talking. If the reader didn't buy the set up, they may never read long enough to get the pay off. Also the piece has a sing song feel that can only come from an ABAB rhyme structure, one that simply wouldn't work in short fiction. Finally, I make use of italics to represent the different speakers, rather than adding dialog tags (the man said, God whispered etc), which if added may have detracted from the piece.

If *Back To Scrolling* was written as a short story, its strength may have been lost. True, I could have told a compelling narrative about a person who has lost everything to their internet addiction, but such a story would be far longer and by necessity included far more than the visceral experience of the poem as it is presented. The first-person narrative, combined with the quick formed thoughts into actions, both serve to replicate a readers real, lived, experience.

Back To Scrolling

Mindless scrolling
Looking for validation online
Filling the time
Filling the void

Someone just liked my post

Fleeting happiness

Back to scrolling
Change apps
Scrolling again
Change apps back

Another like, but not from someone I like

I'm offended
Comment
I'm offended
Share

I wonder what she's doing?
Damn, she's still happy with him

Food as art
Bodies as art
Life as art
How unattainable
I'm jealous

You have memories from seven years ago
Cringe

10 things you won't believe
10 times they got it wrong
10 posts to distract you from your own existence

Screen time report
Usage up from last week

Porn
Porn
Porn
Shame
Close all open tabs
Delete the latest hour

Half formed thought
Tweet
OMG, a retweet!
Just a bot

Bad news
More bad news
Memes about the news
Memes about memes
Sharing memes

I should work
Scroll
I should clean
Scroll
I should exercise
Scroll
I need to sleep

Scroll

Check one app
Check another
Check a third app
Recheck the first

Back to scrolling

What Someone Will Value tells the story of someone reclaiming their worth after a breakup via a collection of statements directed at that person. You learn a lot about the narrator, particularly their evolving views of themselves and of their ex-partner. Once again, the same 'story' could be written as short fiction, a novella, or as a subplot within a larger work. All of those variations are valid and would likely work well. That said, since we are writing a 'story' in the medium of poetry, we need to strip away all the superfluous parts without stripping away the core thrust of the piece.

What Someone Will Value

Don't cry for me
Now that you know
Exactly what you've lost

You chose
To leave

You chose
To burn the bridge

You chose
To turn your eyes elsewhere

Your tears
They tell me
That you failed
To find
Who you were looking for

That she
Wasn't all
She pretended to be

I
Will not
Be a mere
Consolation prize

I am
What someone
Will value

Summary

Good art moves people emotionally – that is why we consume it; we want to be changed in some way. The specific mechanisms of doing so differ depending on the medium. If you are going to use your poetry to tell a story, carefully consider the aspects specific to story: plot, characters, setting and so on. Take the reader on a journey, allow them to learn and grow along with the characters.

Play With Opposites & Subvert Expectations

One way to leave a lasting impression on the reader is to play with opposites and subvert expectations. This will take many different forms, but the basic suggestion would be to twist tried and tested tropes. Turning them on their head and making them mean the opposite of their original meaning, or something new entirely. Surprises, when pulled off well, have added impact due to the shock value.

In *Nightmares & Fantasies* I wanted to highlight how the juxtaposition of opposites can be arousing and flirtatious. Typically, when we read poetry about romance or attraction and the like, we find over the top statements of emotionality or promises of love. Grand declarations of feelings and promises of what one will or has done for another. I wanted to subvert that trope by adding some darkness and ambiguity to

116

the mix. When this is combined with the contrasting themes of darkness and light, the result is compelling indeed.

Nightmares & Fantasies

I am
The intersection
Between your nightmares
And fantasies

Punishing you
With the pleasure
You thought you wanted
Pleasing you
With the pains
You never imagined

I am
Too much
Of a good thing
And
Not enough
Of a bad

Excessive desires
Fulfilled
Scant nourishments

Withheld

Far too much
Of what you want
Not nearly enough
Of what you need

An attractive horror show
Filled
With the bastard children
Of
Ecstasy and terror

In *The Candle Burns* I wanted to play with the saying 'don't burn the candle at both ends', but also consider what the candle itself is giving/sacrificing for us. We don't usually consider the inner world of a candle; it is a mere tool. Yet, as this poem shows us, doing so can be quite moving indeed.

The Candle Burns

The candle burns
Giving light
Giving warmth

By fulfilling its function
It destroys itself

By destroying itself
It serves others

The candle burns
Sacrificing itself
For us

In *Enlightenment* I get meta, addressing the reader directly, and acknowledging within the poem that what is being read is a poem; breaking the fourth wall so to speak. This poem has layers, as it alludes to the authors (my) failings, as the reader's potential for similar failings. It subverts expectations as it isn't normal for poems to be self-referential.

Enlightenment

Social media
Has us believing
That each
And every thought
That crosses our mind
Is such divinely inspired
Wisdom
That it simply must
Be shared
For the sake of the world

The thought
That inspired
This very poem
Is no exception

So tell me
How does
Enlightenment feel?

    I approach subverting expectations and playing with opposites differently with *The Love I Feel*. You can read the strike-through lines alone, the normal lines alone, and then both together. You will notice the flipping and twisting of the rhymes used adds weight to the twisting of the messaging between the two different versions of the poems.

The Love I Feel

~~The love I feel~~
~~So impossibly real~~

The love that's real
So impossible to feel

~~A point of reality~~
~~Against a bleak totality~~

A bleak totality
Devoid of reality

~~A pinprick of light~~
~~That illuminates the night~~

A dark night
Pricked with terror and flight

~~A whispered prayer~~
~~Promising a truth and a dare~~

A violent glare
Promising pain and a scare

~~A look and a touch~~
~~That's never too much~~

A look and a touch
That's always too much

~~A lifetime together~~
~~Souls entwined forever~~

A lifetime together
Souls enmeshed forever

In *Rewrite The Future* I am purposefully evoking opposites on a conceptual level and use the ABAB structure to present the poem. The result is a piece that is immediately engaging but also worthy of a reread and deeper consideration to fully grasp the meaning.

Rewrite The Future

I'd rewrite the future
To change the past
Pray to Gods I don't believe
To make the moment last

Walking backwards from reality
Barefoot and alone
The shifting sands underneath
Have stopped feeling like home

Pleasure always
Has an aspect of pain
And that pain
Always has an aspect of shame

My mind wanders
Faster than I can walk
I'd take it all back
If only I could talk

Summary

Opportunities to play with opposites and subvert expectations are almost limitless. If you are inspired to write something, but it doesn't quite feel like a full or solid idea, consider twisting it on its head. Change an aspect around, move the lines up and down, alter the perspective, flip the emotionality. Experiment with all the aspects of the piece and perhaps you will craft a more evocative poem.

Make All Your Writing Poetic

Why not practice what you are learning here and in the next sections, in your emails, text messages, social media posts, and all other forms of communication? I am not saying to start emailing the boss in rhyme, or writing the shopping list as a sonnet, but rather to consider each piece of text as an opportunity to practice the craft. Ask yourself, can I say this in a more interesting way? Are some of my words superfluous? Could I choose to use more evocative language here? Would the addition of an analogy, symbolism, or alliteration enhance the piece?

Obviously, each form and medium will have its own expectations and restrictions, and like writing structured poetry, you certainly need to stick to those

123

conventions, but perhaps there are opportunities to enhance your writing and thus practice the craft in other areas of your life. Small repetitions, done daily, will yield massive results.

Consider the following tweet. I could have expressed a similar sentiment any number of ways but instead I chose to evoke a poetic flair:

> "distracted
> by distraction
> from distraction"

Whether or not it turned out better that way is besides the point. I aim to practice writing poetically wherever possible and I encourage you to do the same.

Part 3: Technical Advice

The science of writing and editing…

Show And Tell

Probably the most clichéd and widely spouted piece of writing advice comes in the form of 'show don't tell' - Rather than saying how you feel, instead you should show that emotion with imagery, comparison, symbolism, analogy, or specificity of word choice - This is because in general, people respond far more to emotions felt than emotions told.

Consider the following. I could tell you about how war destroys families and kills the innocent. I could give you statistics that highlight numbers lost and the costs of rebuilding. I could state, factually, the plight of a typical refugee. Would such a description evoke emotions in you? For sure, but probably not anywhere near as much as if I instead showed the following simple scene.

A burnt children's toy lies discarded and forgotten just outside the doorway of a bombed-out home. A man sits rocking, head in hands, muttering to himself...

If you want your poetry to move people, show far more than you tell. In *Life* I evoke the imagery of an ant toiling away on a rock in an abyss at the whim of a distant faceless ruler. I could have told you that I was feeling depressed, overworked, and full of existential dread. But analogy evokes feelings that hit far harder than mere explanations of emotions.

Life

I am just an ant
On a rock
Spinning in the abyss

Trudging through
Yet another day

Doing work
I can't comprehend

At the whim
Of a queen
I'll never meet

In *'fever dreams'* I use water to symbolise the flowing nature of thought; 'ponds', 'thirst', and 'drift'. I combined this with 'fever', 'dreams' and 'consciousness', to evoke the feeling of a mind disintegrating into blissful ignorance. I use water again in *'a waterfall shaping rock'* to show that just as we cannot see the impact of one drop of water, we cannot see the impact of one thought. But over time, collectively, the impact is all too apparent. Once again, had I have told you about the feelings behind these poems rather than showing you, the result would have been stale.

fever dreams

fever dreams
liberate the mind
boundless and edgeless

thoughts flow
skipping between
ponds of reality
no longer constrained
by rationality
i drift
what once thirsted for stability
now wants for nothing
but the pretty colours
that seem to hold
all meaning
within this play
of consciousness

a waterfall shaping rock

thoughts
relentless
a waterfall shaping rock

each drop
trivial
yet collectively
devastating

time
forms ruts
inescapable

consciousness
relentless
a river scarring land

each choice
trivial
yet collectively
devastating

thinking patterns
guiding
future flow

It is important to note that you don't need to invoke symbols or illude to things with analogy to 'show' something in a piece. Consider *ever the hypocrite*, the only descriptive word is 'hypocrite', yet despite this, and its short length, it still evokes a story of sorts.

ever the hypocrite

i
ever the hypocrite
ask of you
something
i'd never do

Finally *How Is It?* uses a very small of words to convey a lot of meaning. It doesn't explicitly state that I was overwhelmed or run down, nor does it state the general displeasure I was feeling about the capitalistic nature of society.

How Is It?

How is it
That all I get
For all my time
Is so little money?

There are of course exceptions to the 'show don't tell' rule, sometimes you will choose to tell rather than show, and if you are actively making this chose, your poetry will benefit enormously.

Telling is far quicker and efficient than showing. How much description would it take for me to effectively show you that I was sad? Imagine how the poem *Sad Zac Is Sad* would read if, rather than telling you that '*Sad Zac is sad, He's feeling bad...*', I instead took the time and words to show you all of those feelings? Not only would the poem be far too long, but more importantly, the entire emotional thrust of the piece would be lost.

Excerpt - Sad Zac is Sad

Sad Zac is sad
He's feeling bad
He's feeling like he's been had
That the times he was glad
And feeling rad
Were in fact just a fad…

Telling at appropriate times also frees the poem to focus on deeper level things as the reader won't be distracted unnecessarily. Almost all of *Not Safe* is telling, yet when all of this telling is taken as a whole, the entire poem shows a level of untold and deep emotionality. Spending the words needed to show how 'I am not safe' and that it's 'not pleasant to be in my company' would detrimentally detract from the crux of the piece.

Not Safe

It's not safe
For me to be alone
But it's not pleasant
To be in my company
So how can I

Ask for you
To waste this day
Comforting me?

Finally, adhering to 'show don't tell' can get ridiculous. Take *crescent moon*. The title and the first line 'tells' you that I am talking about a moon. Imagine the absurd lengths it would take to show the imagery of a moon rather than simply stating it? Granted, this may be something you want to play with, but in most circumstances, you will find yourself showing and telling. It is just a matter of actively choosing when to do one over the other, knowing why you should tell here, and show there.

crescent moon

the moon
a cat's claw
a sharp warning
a new dawn

As with all the advice in this book, there are no hard and fast rules. Poetry is an artform and thus there is no 'right way' to do it, only a way that works for you. Basically, if you want to save time and space on the page, telling is far more effective than showing. Not only does it use less words, but it also opens the piece and allows it's focus point to remain clear. That said, if you only tell, you risk your reader feeling nothing, and if your reader feels nothing, they won't be your reader for long.

Summary

Showing makes the reader *feel* something, it evokes imagery, it moves them. Telling saves time and space on the page, but risks feeling like boring narration.

Less Is Best

The human mind evolved to conserve energy. It doesn't want to waste time trying to interpret ambiguity or confusion. When faced with such, most will give up and move on. This isn't to say that we don't want to be challenged, but rather we want to be challenged in a way that we desire. If the grammar and spelling in this book was off, you wouldn't have read this far, the effort would have been too much. If I used a weird/borderline illegible font to present my poetry, it would never be read. You would take one look at it and move on.

The next time you see advertisements, either in person or online, study the font choice and number of words used. Chances are that it is big, bold, clear, and focused. Marketing agencies know that they have minimal time to attain maximum impact.

Do the same with your writing. **Use as few words as possible to convey meaning.** Remove all loose words. Replace stanzas with sentences, and sentences with words. Cut everything that adds no new information to a sentence. Remove all instances of 'very', replacing them with their single word replacements, eg: 'very big' becomes 'humongous'. Most instances of 'that' can be removed without impacting meaning. Practice with haiku and twitter posts as the restricted nature of the format forces brevity. There is a temptation to over explain yourself. Don't. Trust your reader to get it and allow them to come up with their own meanings.

Initially *Fleeting'* was significantly longer, but subsequently far less powerful, 'When eyes meet for a fleeting moment, the possible futures fractaled outward endlessly…', became:

Fleeting

Eyes meet
A fleeting moment
Futures fractal
Possibilities endless

Turn away
A moment passes

Fading memories
What can never be

I started *remember* with 'and then'. What happened before this instance is irrelevant to the point of the poem and would have distracted and detracted from its power.

remember

and then
you remember
the breath
and the silence
within

All unnecessary words have been cut from the poem *tomorrow*. Nothing more can be cut without altering meaning, nor can anything be added.

tomorrow

i'm borrowing
from tomorrow
to pay
for today

The poem *angry* conveys a message as briefly as possible and thus is quite powerful.

angry

i'm angry
at you
for not being
more
like me

No matter the length of the poem, you want it to be as concise as possible. Consider all the longer poems shared within this book. Hopefully there are no loose words, or unnecessary repetition. Of course, you may want to purposefully repeat a phrase, word, or symbol to convey meaning or drive home a point – as long as it is a conscious choice, you are golden.

Summary
Be brief.

Use 'Dumb' Words

All words are valid, but some words are more appropriate to use than others. Our goal is to write evocative poetry, not to showcase our impressive vocabulary. It may make you feel smarter, but if it unintentionally goes over the reader's head, or worse still, is used incorrectly, it will have the opposite of the desired effect.

The title of this section is purposely facetious but it does serve its purpose. Ideally my poetry can be read and understood (at least in a literal sense) by anyone with a rudimentary grasp of the language. I don't want to have people needing to consult a dictionary or to feel inadequate or demoralised by my work. **I want it to be accessible. That said, I also want it to be precise.** I lean towards the first word that arises – rather than looking for 'more complex' alternatives. The only time I break this rule is when the 'dumb' word doesn't convey the specific meaning I desire. During writing I may use it as a place holder, with a little note to remind me to find a better alternative.

In *tomorrow* I could have replaced 'borrowing' with 'leveraging', 'loaning', 'renting', 'taking', 'obtaining' etc. Whilst these alternatives would suffice, they wouldn't have been as powerful.

tomorrow

i'm borrowing
from tomorrow
to pay
for today

In *a page to listen*, I chose to use the word 'tragic' because it best fits what I was trying to say. Potential (weaker) alternatives include 'sad', 'calamitous', 'awful', 'dire', 'terrible' etc.

a page to listen

my poems
are tragic
so that my life
isn't

i write
to release the demons
i invented
to protect myself

when I had
nothing else
i had a pen to speak
and a page to listen

Conversely, in *Lifeblood* I choose to use the words 'lacerated' and 'writhes', over the simpler options because these evoke imagery in one word, that could otherwise take a sentence, thus contradicting the 'less is best' advice from the previous section. **Choose the best word for the job, regardless of how fancy or common it sounds.**

Lifeblood

Not yet dead
The demon
Writhes
On the page

Lacerated
By the light of attention
It stares
Horrified

As its lifeblood
Becomes the ink
Of its own
Eulogy

Summary

Avoid using fancy words when there is a simpler option. Don't use a thesaurus to insert words you don't know the meaning of. Chances are you will be saying something you aren't fully intending, or else, needlessly complicating your work – Both of which will detract from the readability of the poem.

Tie The Loop

There is a nice feeling of closure that can arise when you end a poem by bringing the reader back to the beginning – this is a common factor in short fiction writing that can also be used to enhance your poetry. This could be accomplished by repeating a core word, rhyme, theme, or symbol. If the poem takes them on a journey, then returning to the beginning acts as a compelling example of contrast. Alternatively, you can tie the loop showing no changes to emphasise the static nature of the emotions or situation of the poem.

In Do *You Love Me, Or Just The Idea Of Me*, I open with the concept of a 'dream girl' and end with '...unless of course, they're just a dream'. I further add to the symbolism with mentions of 'reality', 'fantasy', and 'open your eyes'. Combined, this 'tying of the loop' brings the reader back to the beginning of the poem giving them a feeling of catharsis and completion because they have found themselves back at the beginning – or something like it.

Do You Love Me, Or Just The Idea Of Me?

Do you love me,
Or just the idea of me?

I may be your 'dream girl'
But I am real,
And that reality is different
From your fantasy.

How often must we fight,
Just to clarify
That you expected
Me to speak differently?

How many tears must fall,
Just to realise
That you expected
Me to be something I'm not?

If you love me,
Please drop your expectations
And open your eyes
To the real me.

My body has blemishes.
I will lose my temper.
I judge unfairly.
I get things wrong.

I am not perfect,

No one is.
Unless of course,
They're just a dream.

I demonstrate a simple tying of the loop in *Sorry My Boy* by making the last line reference the reframe, as well as flipping the theme of being too busy on its head with the boy now rejecting the father.

Sorry My Boy

Sorry my boy
I've got something to do
And unfortunately
It doesn't involve you

Sorry my boy
I don't have the time to chat
I'm too busy
But you know that

Sorry my boy
I can't play right now
There is too much on
I've done as much as my schedule will allow

Hey my boy
I'm finally free

Want to hang out
Just you and me?

Sorry my dad
I've got too much on
With my work and my mates
My time's all gone

In very few words, *Work Life Balance* it tells a story that neatly circles back upon itself.

Work Life Balance

Attempting to balance
Work and life
Just seems like another job
I don't have time
To complete

Swallow The Poison touches upon a similar theme to *Work Life Balance* but employs the ABAB rhyme structure, as well as using its length to tell a story. The last stanza directly ties the loop with a rephrasing of the first. The poem also references earlier parts of itself throughout the piece, leading to a powerful and coherent delivery of the core theme and message.

Swallow The Poison

Swallow the poison
Trade your day
Time for money
Life's wasting away

Work to live
Not to thrive
It's all you can do
Just to survive

Take a moment
Look around
This is your life
What have you found?

Your kids are old
Your friends are gone
Your dreams are unmet
But you can't move on

You earn just enough
To cover the bills
You know what would happen
If you took ill

You'd lose your job
And then the house

Then the car
Then the spouse

So every day
No matter what
You swallow your poison
The only hope you've got

To earn enough
To survive the night
And do it all again
The daily fight

Not quite the fairy tale
You were promised in youth
But let's be honest
No-one could accept the truth

It's the daily grind
Called that for a reason
To hope for other wise
Is demonised as treason

We are in this together
The workers plea
Collective repression
Then distracted depravity

Work for the weekend

Then pay to play
Porn, liquor, and drugs
Then some takeaway

It's not in your budget
But you convince yourself it's okay
Cause it's all you can do
To survive another workday

Don't think of the future
It's far to long
30 years more of this
What could possibly go wrong?

But hey!
Doesn't retirement actually seem good?
Finally you have the time needed
To do everything you wish you now could

So you delay gratification
Of most every form of joy
Problem is you'll be too old by then
To enjoy it anyway

Still you delude yourself
It's part of the poison
Swallowing your dreams
Then acting with caution

Besides those weekend benders
Leave you with little spare wealth
With little motivation
With diminishing health

You sometimes wonder
How you ended up here
Overwhelmed by resentment
You crack another beer

'It is what it is'
'Inflation is high'
'It's capitalisms fault'
To yourself you justify

There goes the weekend
It's time for another dose
Off to work again
Hunting that promotion grandiose

A different brand of poison
A variation of the old promise
You'll get paid far more
Cause you're no longer a novice

In your new role
You think you will finally be free
Until it dawns on you
All that extra responsibility

Even less time
For those that you love
For the friends you don't see
For all the hobbies you let go of

But what other choice
Could you realistically pursue?
If you changed path now
Only chaos would ensue

So you swallow the poison
You trade your day
Exchanging time for money
Letting your life waste away

Unlike art, life is full of loose ends and unanswered questions. Think of everyone you have ever known and consider how many questions you still have. True, you might 'not care' in the grand scheme of things, but you cannot deny that knowing those answers would add *something* to your life. Perhaps it isn't important enough to actively pursue the answers to, but you wouldn't say no to knowing – this is why gossip is so intriguing by the way. **The good news is that you can answer those questions for your readers and some poems will benefit from doing so.** They will feel more complete, more 'right'. Similarly, if you return to the same themes, the poem will feel more internally consistent – this is important as it makes the entire piece feel like it belongs with itself.

Summary
Tying the loop makes your whole piece feel internally consistent – returning back to elements of symbolism, word choice, story, or rhyme can feel better for the reader.

Repetition & 'The Rule Of 3'

Extending on the previous section, the repetition of words, rhymes, sounds, meanings, and symbolism can make a piece pop. Experiment with groups of three as they tend to sound extra enticing.

In *Seed* I repeatedly use the dual rhyme endings of 'eed' and 'urt', the symbolism of seeds and pain, as well as the use of the same words in the penultimate paragraph in a different context from their first mention to evoke an alternative meaning. Finally, I also 'tie the loop' with a reintroduction of 'seed' at the end.

Seed

Sometimes,
I feel like a seed.

A potential inert,
A possibility to succeed.
So just put me in the dirt
And give me what I need.
How else can I avert?
How else can I exceed?

Other times,
I feel hurt.
Just a societal weed.
A potential victim on alert,
Nurtured only when I bleed.
I don't mean to be curt,
How else can I plead?
How else can I divert?
How else can I be freed?

I am the hurt seed, the weed that's only freed by the
blood that it bleeds. Put into the dirt just wishing to
exceed. Inert without encouragement, unable to
succeed. Thus, I plead; Be alert to my need. Don't
divert or think me curt, I just want to succeed.

So just bury me
And perhaps this seed
Will grow
Into a weed.

In 'A Moment Fragmented' I use many repetitions

of the same words, 'Forever', 'Another', and 'Just', as well as employ the rule of 3 by using alliteration with 'Replayed, rewound, and reworked'.

A Moment Fragmented

A moment fragmented
Against a lifetime
Of similar moments

A life shattered
Well before it's time

Those moments
Replayed, rewound, and reworked

Those moments reconstructed
Into a tolerable shadow

Forever following
Forever protecting
Forever warning

Forever recalling
Those moments
Where life was fragmented

Forever forestalling

Advancement and growth

Forever focusing
Upon the past
And everything it implies
About the future

Another moment
Another fragmentation
Another destruction
Another shadow
Another protection
Another warning
Another follower

Just more weight
To carry into the future
Just more weight
To hold me in place
Just more weight
To remember

Just more
Just another

Just me
Reliving a moment

All those moments

Again

Finally, in *I Took It For Granted*, I take the concept of repetition and the rule of 3 to the extreme with multiple examples of each.

I Took It For Granted

My body was broken,
before I realised it was my own.

I took it for granted,
while it was slowly being taken.

I used it without thought,
I used it without comprehension,
I used it without appreciation.

Now it's just used.

I got old,
before I realised I was ageing.

I squandered what I had,
while worrying about what I would become.

I wasted my time,
I wasted my energy,

I wasted my opportunity.

Now I'm just wasted.

My life was over,
before I realised I was living it.

I ignored reality,
but reality kept a watch on me.

I spent my time,
I spent my money,
I spent my soul.

Now I'm just spent.

Once you start looking for repetition of threes in writing you won't be able to stop noticing them, they are everywhere, and for good reason – they enhance writing. Obviously it is a matter of preference, but take a look at the above poems again, and remove one instance of a three (or add one to make it four). Would that change make the poem better? Personally, I don't think so.

Summary
Repetition, particularly in groups of three, can enhance poetry and your writing in general.

Play With Presentation

Consider how you want the poem to 'look' on the page. Make an active choice about its alignment, paragraph structure, title, and the use of capitalisations and grammar (or lack thereof). You are the artist and therefore you will want the words on the page to transmit to the reader in a certain way. These choices help to make that happen – of course, the reader is free to take your work however they like! **Just be internally consistent within the poem.**

Compare the poems presented within this book and you will see that each one is purposefully presented to convey a particular meaning, emotion, or point. Had I formatted them all the same way, some of the impact and meaning would have been lost, thus weakening those pieces. Unless you are creating poetry that follows an established, predetermined structure, you are 'free' to present it however you like. Do not take this to mean that you can just mindlessly slap some amazing imagery on a page and expect it to be appreciated. Presentation matters. Take *a page to listen*, below I will present it as intended, and then I will present a few more times with different formatting – you will quickly see how doing so changes the piece entirely.

a page to listen

my poems
are tragic
so that my life
isn't

i write
to release the demons
i invented
to protect myself

when I had
nothing else
i had a pen to speak
and a page to listen

Reformatted #1

My poems are tragic so that my life isn't. I write to release the demons I invented to protect myself. When I had nothing else, I had a pen to speak and a page to listen.

Reformatted #2

my poems are tragic
so that my life isn't

i write to release the demons
i invented to protect myself

when I had nothing else
i had a pen to speak and a page to listen

I could go on with the different reformatting attempts, but it's clear that looks matter. The line breaks imply a slight pause in thought and emphasis. The use of grammar informs how the poem should sound when spoken and read, and the purposeful choice to not use grammar implies other things. **Before your poem is complete, make sure that you've considered more than just the words you are using, but also how those words are presented on the page, and of course, how that presentation will impact how it would be spoken if read out loud (or as the reader's inner voice).** Thus, if you want them to 'get' the cadence of the poem you have written in a certain way, make sure it is presented that way. **If you aren't sure, read it out loud, or better still, get a trusted friend to do so (without prior prompting) and just listen to how your poem sounds, based on how it is written. Tweak the presentation accordingly.**

Summary
The presentation of a poem impacts how it is perceived and how it will be received.

Tips For Titles

You want to carefully consider the name of your poem. Often the name will come from a word or a line within the poem that best exemplifies its meaning. You want to choose a word or phrase that is catchy and symbolic. Consider the names of most of the poems presented in this book and you will see that I usually adhere to this rule. That said, I chose the title for *Dad* because I wanted to use the title to contextualise the meaning of the poem to the reader – but I felt that attempting to cram the word *'dad'* into the poem would make it feel clunky and forced.

Dad

What thoughts
Are confined
In the vault
Of your mind?

Why
Don't you speak
And share
What you think?

I don't know
Who you are
Beyond what
I can see

And what I can see
Is that you
Clearly
Have no time for me

Of course, given the free nature of poetry, there are no limitations to what you can and cannot do when naming a piece. Some poets choose to put the name of their piece after the poem. This option can emphasise certain points of the piece, or recontextualise aspects of the piece, causing the reader to reconsider the whole. Consider the following small example:

all words
are just air
through meat

broken promises

The poem itself could be interpreted multiple ways, but the addition of the title at the end, which doesn't come from inside the piece, has the effect of reframing it into a story of despondency and disappointment, perhaps implying the breakdown of a relationship. Had the title been at the start, perhaps the entire piece would be less evocative.

In *look at what i overcame,* I also place the title at the end of the poem, which adds a level of ambiguity that enhances the impact of the title and thus the piece as a whole. Is the title yet another statement from a belligerent relative berating the author, or is it the author highlighting what they themselves overcame? In this way, the title is now more than a mere label, it itself has become part of the poem.

hide your shame
don't share your pain
why'd you bring it up again?
you're the one with blame
i told you it was just a game
you must be insane
you must be lame
I can't believe the lies you claim
i can't believe the failure you became
i can't believe we share the same name

look at what i overcame

Of course, poems do not need to be named. Once again, this choice will have its own positives and negatives. Not giving it a name suggests mystery, freedom, and choice of the reader to take it wherever it takes them. That said, it does take away the opportunity to frame the piece or add something extra to it. Also, not having a title, makes it more difficult for readers to talk about the piece – if you plan on sharing your work with the world and want to grow an audience, you may want to consider the impacts of unnamed pieces on SEO, contents pages, and other digital marketing impacts. Not very poetic, but for some of you it will be a pivotal consideration.

Summary
Choosing a name for your poem is an opportunity to add or expand upon the piece – as is the placement of the name – it is just as much a part of the piece as the words within.

Find A Good Editor & Listen To Their Advice

Sometimes we are simply too close to our work to be able to see it for what it is. Perhaps the subject matter is too emotional, or the writing process was too taxing. Maybe our egos are over inflated and are not allowing us to see the flaws. Our self-worth might be down and we are doubting our ability to create anything of value. Or perhaps another set of eyes could solve the problems we cannot even see.

In a previous section I discussed the concept of splitting the creative and editing into different roles to ensure that you get out of your own way and just write. This is vital as you cannot be effectively doing both creation and editing at the same time. Despite this split, and even with a time delay, it can still be hard to detach yourself enough from the process to see your work for what it is. This is where an editor can come in handy. For poetry, I use my wife for this purpose who, for the most part, tweaks some grammar here and there and ticks my poetry off as great. She often is a cheerleader when she sees I need it and highlights potential changes when appropriate. Every now and then however she tells me I can do better, or that a poem isn't done yet, or that it isn't good enough. It stings, but I have learnt to trust her. Because she is right. The most poignant example of this comes from the poem *Can't Quite Express* – a mono-rhyming poem I wrote seven years ago. It was a mere 128 words and at the time I felt it aptly expressed what I felt I couldn't express (the irony of the title was intended). She helped me to whittle down this poem to be lean, cutting, and poignant, and then approved it. However, seven years later, I returned to the poem, extending it to 1261 words, believing that perhaps the poem had evolved into 6 minute spoken word 'song'. Once again, we went through the editing process, tweaking and fixing it. Nonetheless, the result still didn't feel quite right, and another 245 words came. **I thought I was done, but she told me it wasn't. She still felt like there was more - and well, she was right.** Over the next few days, *Can't Quite Express* became a 6704-word epic poem, that I ended up publishing as a standalone book. Without her prompting, I would never have completed it – or even known of its existence within me. She helped me cut the longer form of poem down by a quarter, highlighting problematic verses, as well as things that didn't quite fit with the rest of the piece. Acting as my editor, she pulled it out of me, prompting me to do more, highlighting where I could do better, guiding the process, and suggesting areas that weren't working. **The result is far better than I ever could have created on my own.**

Can't Quite Express (original)

There are things I want to say
But just can't quite express
Ruminations and meditations
I'm too afraid to address
Like the veil over my eyes
That keeps me hidden from the stress
To the dark wishes
I'm fighting to suppress
Like the fear and anxiety
That I will constantly transgress
To the past expressions
I am never going to confess
Like how everything I do

Gives me nothing but duress
To the unwavering ache and torment
That's causing me to regress

I must profess
I desire to express my stress
Confess to address this abscess
To obsess on happiness
To aim for excess
And to stop living like a fucked-up mess

Yes
I want to make progress
But there are just some things I can't quite express

I am blessed to live with my chosen editor, but that comes with some potential issues. I have had to train myself in how to best receive feedback and her on how to best give it (tips below). Your editor may be a friend, a family member, an online connection, or paid help. Find someone who you can both work with, and importantly hear negative feedback from whilst maintaining the relationship. I have been writing for years and it is still hard not to take it personally. I know she isn't criticising me but nonetheless it can still feel like it. Those feelings, whilst valid, have no place in the process. And as such need to be managed. To this end, I have now also started branching out and receiving help from friends and fellow writers, all who provide me with different kinds of advice and feedback, all of which I am extremely grateful for.

Share the following advice with your editor, so they know how to give feedback, and what to expect from you during the process:

Tips on receiving feedback:

When receiving feedback, be quiet and listen. Don't comment until they have finished expressing their opinion. Don't defend your work or justify why you made the choices that you made. Just listen.

Once you have heard them out, ask specific questions. What did you think of this part? How did it make you feel? Were there any areas that didn't work? Why? Did you notice any loose/wasted words. Is it finished?

If you want cheerleading, ask for it. Just know that if you do, you cannot also get constructive criticism at the same time. If needed, tell your editor to give you 'the shit sandwich' – praise, critique, praise. This approach makes it easier to manage the emotions that can arise. Alternatively, let them know you need to be told that your effort/intentions are good (cheerleading), but you would like specific help to make your work better.

Remember that it isn't their job to write or even fix the poem. They are just there to highlight potential issues that you may not be aware of. It is your job to fix the issue.

You, the writer, choose when and how to take the advice of the editor. Ultimately it is your work, and thus your decision as to how the completed piece should look.

Thank them for giving feedback – navigating the emotions of a poet can be hard, and even if you are paying them, they still should be thanked!

Tips on giving feedback:

Don't give unasked for feedback – even if you have worked with them before. Wait until they ask for your services before you offer your opinion.

Ask if they want critique or cheerleading. Sometimes your writer will just want praise for doing a good job, if so, give it to them. Just make sure that you are clear that the cheerleading isn't a critique.

Don't (at least initially) attempt to 'fix' the work or offer suggestions. This may make the poet change the piece to suit your ideas, not theirs. They are the writer, not you. A better approach is to share what you felt whilst reading. What parts jumped out at you? What parts emotionally moved you? Bored you? Confused you? Show them how you felt and let them tweak the piece to address those feelings - then repeat until the piece shines.

Only give feedback on things you are competent at/are asked for, eg: if you don't know how to copy edit, don't offer to do it!

Remember that the editing process is ongoing and often takes multiple attempts before the poem is at a 'publishable standard'. Some of the poems within this book were fine upon first writing, others took over ten iterations to get it right. It is important to be patient, both with yourself and your editor. If your editor is telling you that something isn't working and you cannot figure it out then and there, that is okay. Put the piece down and work on something else for a while. Perhaps with fresh eyes you will be able to fix the problem.

I adhere to the adage that **80% is done**. Don't get me wrong, I want to make my work perfect, but I know the risk of the attempt. Firstly, it is impossible to achieve perfection – by my own or anyone's standard. Secondly, I know that the attempt will hamper my overall writing career. I could have rewritten the first chapter of my first book again and again. In fact, I could still be doing so. That chapter would have been amazing, and undoubtedly better than it currently is, but if I had done that, I wouldn't be writing this book, nor would I have learnt the many lessons along the way that my later work gave me.

Summary

166

Perfection is in the process, not in the final product. Write the poem and then edit the poem – potentially with the help of another person. Then write a new poem. Repeat.

Sleep On It

Sometimes I will 'finish' a poem, but I won't be totally satisfied with the result. Something feels off. Incomplete. Forced. Contrived. Or just not 'me'. When this happens, I sleep on it – literally. I will save the poem and return to it the next day and take another go at it. Often I find that there is something wrong with the meaning, the word choices, the layout, the grammar, or the flow. Most of the time all I need is one day, but sometimes a poem needs weeks, or in the case of *Can't Quite Express* (above) seven years.

The break allows your mind to reset and refocus. It is a way to force yourself to detach from the poem and then to see it in a new light. Just one night may be enough to fix those unexplainable issues you feel about your work. If, after a day or so, you haven't made any changes, chances are that the negative feelings about your poem is coming from an issue of self-worth or confidence about yourself, rather than an issue with your current poem. **If you have made changes and are still not totally happy, perhaps a longer break from the poem is necessary for you**

to get the needed level of detachment to identify and fix it.

I wrote the poem *souls entwined* and felt it was done - almost. It was projecting the message and feeling that I wanted to express, it was tying the loop with the phrase 'escape their fate' and had multiple uses of the rule of 3. But something was off, and I couldn't quite place it. So, I put the poem away and came back to it the following night, rewording and renaming it to *escape their fate*. You can decide which version is 'better' but personally I like the latter. It feels less forced, less contrived and has a different flow. I feel like it tells a more real story and projects its core meaning better.

souls entwined

souls entwined
same trauma
same pain
same desire to escape their fate

ancestors collectively mourning
lost childhoods
lost freedoms
lost innocence

drawn together

shared suffering
shared knowledge
shared hopes

desperately praying
for a better future
for a break in the cycle
for their children to escape their fate

escape their fate

souls entwined
with a desire
to escape their fate

ancestors
collectively mourning
lost childhoods

disparate people
drawn together
by shared suffering

stumbling
forward
into a new life

fleeing their pasts

unwittingly creating
their futures

they know
what not to do
but not what to do

attempting to avoid
the same mistakes
their parents made

desperately praying
for their children
to escape their fate

Almost all work benefits from the detached perspective granted by sleeping on it. That said, **it isn't always advisable to make extensive changes to a piece after the fact**. Creativity is often purest in its initial moments. Take too long to return to a piece and you may find that it feels stale or somehow off – chances are that feeling is arising because you are no longer in the same headspace you were when you created it.

Summary
If you are struggling to finish a piece take some time away from it before returning with fresh eyes.

Part 4: Writing Activities

Practice makes perfect…

What follows are some activities to help you begin or enhance your writing process. I suggest that you don't just read what follows, but actually give the activities a try. I have put these here for a reason – they work. They won't all work for you, but some certainly will. It would be a shame for you to miss out on adding a vital tool to your writing arsenal. I state this here because I know how easy it is to read ideas from a book, to promise yourself that you will do it, and then promptly forget. So, try these activities, your writing will thank you - but be smart, if you are doing one of these activities and discover that an evocative poem of your own is desperate to be written, stop the activity and write that poem. Remember, we are trying to both inspire creativity in the moment, but also give you the tools to combat writer's block and inspire new and alternative methods of expression.

Sit In Silence

Technology has granted us the ability to have endless distraction. Videos, podcasts, social media, books, messages, memes, and more. It is possible to literally spend every waking moment with some kind of input coming in. This isn't natural and isn't conducive to creativity. I've spoken to thousands of people on this topic, with most saying they are afraid of silence. They struggle to believe that they could sit alone with their thoughts for longer than a minute. Some doubt they'd last even that long. Whilst I have said elsewhere that it is important to get inspiration from multiple sources, it is important to allow said inspiration to work its magic and have some space to inspire you.

That space is silence.

Whilst it is possible to create while simultaneously consuming media, it isn't easy. Ideas are like delicate seedlings attempting to burst through the dirt and establish themselves. They are small, they are quiet, they are easily destroyed. But, if you give them the gift of silence, they can thrive.

Activity – 20 Minutes Of Silence

Get a timer and something to write on. If you choose something digital, make sure to set it to do not disturb, and have the writing application open and ready. Set a timer for 20 minutes and wait. Let your thoughts flow. Let yourself become lost in them. Do not force yourself down any one path, rather imagine the thoughts that come as cars on a road. You are simply observing them pass. When a strong idea comes, one that seems like it simply *must* be written down, do so. Feel free to continue writing on this idea beyond the 20 minutes if needed. If however, you start writing and the idea falls away, don't force it, instead let it go and return to observing the thoughts for the remainder of the time.

Limit Yourself

A blank page is intimidating. It could be filled with anything, but right now, it is filled with nothing. Ahhhhhhhh! Not only do you have to write something on that page, but you also must choose what will be written, and then you must make it 'good' – whatever that means.

For better or worse, you are free. Sometimes it can be hard to know what to do, as the page can literally have anything on it. Thus, you restrict your options to increase creativity. This sounds counter-intuitive, surely having more choices would allow for more creativity, right? Sometimes, but often not. If you limit your options, you may find that those limitations enhance your creativity. You now need to create something glorious, within the bounds of certain barriers. These barriers could be imposed by you, made up in the moment, and be as loose or as tight as you like. Or they could be the restrictions imposed by following a traditional structure. You will notice in previous sections I talk about different structures, both formal and my own, that I chose to write under. This is no accident. Sometimes I chose to write a piece with a particular restriction in place, other times the piece was coming and with it, the certain restrictions that I wanted it to fit.

Here are a few potential restrictions to consider and try:

'ABAB'

The ending word of the second and fourth sentences rhyme, this could be implemented for one or more stanzas (paragraphs) or extended into an 'English Sonnet' with the ABAB CDCD EFEF GG structure.

Example of ABAB:

Excessive Thinking

I replaced
Drinking
With excessive
Thinking

The hangover
Is worse
Thoughts
Form a curse

No longer

Dumb
No longer
Numb

Swallow burn
Shame
Write ink
Pain

Bottles
Emptied of sin
Notepads
Fill the bin

Addicted
To stress
Addicted
Nonetheless

The bar
Is locked
My writing
Is blocked

My 12 step
Process
Is
Journaling this nonsense

Just these few
Lines
Stress and whiskey
Rhymes'

Should I have
Another?
Write on my
Brother!

'Mono-Rhyme'
The ending word of each sentence has the same rhyme sound, and/or the same rhyming sound is used throughout the entirety of the poem. This can be hypnotic to hear and impactful to analyse – particularly given the potential need for obscure words to be used to maintain both the rhyme and 'story' of the poem.
Example:

Spilled Ink

Spilled ink
Words to make you think
Words to drink
Words to talk you back from the brink
Words written to your shrink
It's okay
I too am out of sync

Struggling with the link
Between my kink
And those who chose to hoodwink
Clearly I need to rethink
Cause life is over in a blink
And I've got no more time for their stink

'Haiku'
The haiku structure: 5, 7, 5 syllables, is a great way to practice brevity and word choice. Traditionally Haiku are written about nature, but you can use the structure to talk on anything.
Example:

Trapped

I find myself trapped
By the very rituals
I made to survive

'Alliteration'
Alliteration when you use the same starting letter of two or more words in a sentence. Either changing the letter choice each sentence/stanza or keeping that same letter for the entire poem.
Examples:

Defecation As Distraction

From the seclusion
of our toilets
We like the curated lies
of another's life

As our bowels open up
Shit flows from our fingertips

As we wipe
We swipe right

As we flush
We consume content

As we wash
We scroll

Urination as unity
Defecation as distraction
Expulsion as expression

Stupefied

I sit
Stupefied
Seeking solace

From shame

The silence
Is no longer safe
Secrets seep
From the shadow

Slowly I find myself
Surrounded
My sanity siphoned
Into stillness

Activity – Limit Yourself, Part 1

Pick one of the following topics to write upon: grief, betrayal, lust, dread, love, peace. Then attempt to write a poem on that topic using **each** of the four restrictions discussed above: ABAB, mono-rhyme, haiku, and alliteration. For the mono-rhyme, use the ending sound of the topic word to base the rest of the poem off, eg: 'love' – 'dove' – 'glove'. For the alliteration restriction, use the first letter of topic word to base the rest of the poem off, eg: 'love' – 'lemon' – 'lake'. These poems do not have to be 'good'. This activity is designed to show you that perhaps restrictions can inspire creativity and help you to fill the blank page.

There are plenty more traditional styles of poetry for you to explore, as well as many other ways you could think to limit yourself. If you take another look at the poems I have shared throughout this book, you will notice that some of them follow their own internally consistent rules. Maybe I wanted to use the same phrase repeatedly, perhaps I wanted the tenses to change, maybe I wanted certain symbols to be featured, or perhaps I wanted the poem to 'look' a certain way on the page. The point is, you may discover that by imposing rules upon yourself aka, making it 'harder' to write the poem, you are boosting your creativity and thus the impact of the poem.

Activity – Limit Yourself, Part 2

Take the same topic you chose for part 1 and write a new poem. But before (or as) you do, impose your own unique rule upon the poem, eg: restricting the syllables used in each line, ending each line with the topic word, doing a reverse mono-rhyme where each lines starting word rhymes, making the poem make sense when written forwards and backwards. This rule can be anything, so get creative and make it a challenge.

Sometimes it is important to break the rules. I find that it can help to write a poem under certain structures or self-imposed rules, but as I am finishing the poem, find it useful to break those rules to add some extra impact to the piece. If the reader is expecting a certain thing, then breaking those expectations can be evocative. That said, it also can cause the piece to suffer, so be careful!

Don't (Always) Limit Yourself

Some poetry will be best written 'free form'. That is, no structure, no rhyme, no rules. Just words on a page. Sometimes these poems work best when left alone, presented as they come. Others may need some tweaking or tightening up. Others still would benefit from the application of some of the technical advice contained within this book – retroactively altering the structure and contents to make it 'pop'. Knowing what to do and when is the artform. A skill that you will be able to hone with practice and experimentation.

Empty doesn't follow any of the rules I have discussed, other than line breaks, brevity, and consistent theme. I used my intuition and experience to choose the words and the line breaks, and I slept on it to revise. Many of the other poems in this book started in a similar fashion, but I felt they needed to 'tie the loop' or would benefit from the introduction of 'the rule of 3', or that alliteration felt like it needed to be added. Once again, practice will hone your intuition on when and what changes to make.

empty

sitting
in the sun
in an empty field
my head
too heavy to hold
i numbly
weep
for the life
i was too afraid
to live

I take a lack of limits even further in *a sentence without grammar* completely discarding grammar, capitalisations, and even a resolution to the poem – all of which is done to enhance the meaning that is at the core the piece.

a sentence without grammar

i feel like a sentence
without grammar

perfectly legible
yet nonetheless
fundamentally lacking
something
everyone else seems
to have

i feel like a poem
that lacks a rhyme

capable
of functioning
to a high degree
yet nevertheless
unappealing
to the masses

i feel like a story
that was left unfinished

interesting
but ultimately
...

Activity – No Limits

Find a place of solitude and spend some time
settling into the space. Take some slow calming

breaths, get comfortable, and get yourself prepared to write. Then simply sit and listen to the sounds that arise. You are not aiming to rush or force anything. But when you feel the urge, write. Do not worry about the final product; it doesn't matter how it sounds, if it is good, or even if it makes sense. Just get the words onto the page. Then, once you have written, look over your words, asking yourself if there is a potential poem in there.

Can you tweak the writing as is with line breaks and other poetic tools to form a poem?

Are there any themes, imagery, or symbolism you want to explore?

Has something related (or not related) arrived that simply needs to be written?

If you answer yes to any of those questions, write!

Write Like X

Analysing another's work and attempting to replicate it can provide useful insights and skills. I am not saying that you should imitate another's style and make it your own, as doing so would likely result in a stale, uninspired, or clichéd piece of art. What I am saying is that there are significant lessons to be learnt from studying how other people write. If you are moved by their work, it would be wise to work out why. Rather than just reading the work, study it. Perhaps you will notice certain phrases, stylistic choices, beats, grammatical quirks, and other subtleties. Maybe you will then see opportunities to implement a version of this into your work. Remember, it may have already been said or done, but not by you. Do not stress if initially your writing seems to be a poor imitation of someone else. Just keep writing and expand your study to other poets and forms of inspiration. Eventually you will naturally integrate certain aspects of others work whilst simultaneously creating poetry that is uniquely your own.

Activity – Rewrite A Poem

Take any poem that you enjoy and rewrite it word for word.

Literally copy it down onto the page as it was originally presented. This will give you a real *feel* for how the poet crafted their work. You are literally writing what they wrote and by doing so, you are forced to pay far more attention to the word choice, structure, grammar etc than you would had you merely read it. This hyper focus will help you to integrate their style into your own, and thus inspire your future work.

Activity – Reform A Poem

Take the poem you chose above and reform it.

Reread each line and change some of the words, tweak its structure, play with its grammar. Your goal is to reform it so that what you create is like the original poem, but from another dimension. Similar meaning, similar style, similar words, just slightly *altered*. Be as subtle or as bold as you like. This will show you how small choices can impact the totality of the poem. It will reveal that the original poets' choices are just one of many possibilities of how the poem *could have* been written. It will show you that perhaps your unique creativity has value – even when playing within such a limited scope.

Activity – Respond To A Poem

Once again, take that same poem and this time respond to it.

Using the same structure and rules of the poem (if it has them) write your own poem about, or in response to, the original. You can retell the poem in your own words, express how you felt whilst reading, or use symbolism and memories from your own experiences to project the same emotionality and sentiment of the original. Once again, we are not aiming for a masterpiece here, just wanting to use

186

another's work as a starting point/catalyst for your own creativity.

Rhyme Time

At the time of writing my eldest son is six years old. To keep him entertained during long car rides we play 'Rhyme Time'. The rules are simple, I say a word, and he responds with a word that rhymes with it, then I give another, and he gives another. We continue until no more rhymes are given. He then chooses a new word, and the game begins again.

Eg: red, bed, head, shed etc

When this got too easy, the game evolved into 'Rhyme Time Story Mode' where instead of just saying rhyming words, they must be put into a sentence.

Eg: I bumped my head getting out of my red bed in the rush to get to my shed.

My hope is that I will be able to evolve this game further to include alliteration, emotionality, and eventually on the spot ABAB poem creations.

Eg:

I cannot complain
For I still have my head
Despite what was forgotten
Upon rising from my bed

Activity – Rhyme Time

For each of the following words, note down some rhymes. Put two or more into a simple sentence. Then into an ABAB structured poem.

1: 'Creation'
2: 'Show'
3: 'Good'

You can do this game any time you like, with a partner or on your own. Just look around the room, consider your thoughts, or respond to a choice word you have read. This activity will get you flexing your rhyme muscles. The more repetitions, the stronger you will become.

Word Association

Another great way to warm up the creative parts of your mind is to play with word associations – basically this involves exploring the first thoughts that pop into your mind, in response to a prompt.

Activity – Word Association

Below, you will find a list of words. I want you to read each one in turn, and instantly respond to them. Say or write down the first thing that comes to mind. Some words will be positive, some neutral, and some potentially negative. The idea is that we are just learning how to quickly respond to certain concepts and words, and in doing so getting out of our own way/turning off the internal editor. Remember, there are no wrong answers. All you need to do is respond with the first thing that arises.

1: Strength
2: Fun
3: Love
4: Family
5: Hate
6: The past
7: Success
8: Pain
9: Relaxation
10: Life
11: Pleasure
12: The future
13: Home

Prime The Pump

A part of creativity involves 'priming the pump'. Have you ever seen a hose or pump being used for the first time in a while? It needs to be primed - used a bit before the water flows cleanly. At first the debris comes shooting out, quickly followed by the brown disgusting water. But eventually, the flow runs pure, and the water is drinkable. The writing analogy suggests that we need to 'prime the pump' of our writing wells – basically spending some time at the start of each writing session just writing whatever crap we need to allow the good stuff to flow through us and onto the page.

Hidden at the back of a drawer, beside my

writing desk, is a pile of 10 or more discarded notepads. Each one is full of ramblings, journal entries, nonsensical/half formed thoughts and poems that went nowhere. Apparently I needed to write all of that before I could write anything I felt comfortable enough to commit to finishing, let alone sharing. The scary thing for me is looking at all of that 'wasted' writing, knowing that I could have easily quit because I wasn't doing anything of 'worth'. True, the contents themselves aren't worth anyone reading, but the act of writing them was vital for me to be writing these words now. The same is true for my poetry. Often it will take a few false starts and a lot of extra words before the 'true poem' reveals itself or allows itself to be written. If I was to force the work, or stop before the pump was fully primed, the poems would never have come!

Activity – Prime The Pump

Set a timer for 5 minutes and start writing.

Don't worry about spelling, grammar, editing, audience, or anything. Just write. Your goal is to get words onto the page – without judgement or filter. If you need help starting, write the following line and continue from there,

'I am doing the 'prime the pump' activity as a way to

191

start the words flowing onto the page, I have chosen to start like this because I didn't know how else to start this process, but now as I write these words, I am noticing some emotions, thoughts, feelings, images and memories arising, I will write these down now…'

As always, if this activity causes a piece of poetry or other writing to come, keep going beyond the 5 minutes, but whatever you do, don't stop early!

Activity – Journaling As Writing Therapy

Journaling could be done as a single session, each day, as an additional way to 'prime the pump'. I have found benefits of journaling as a part of my morning or night-time routine, or prior to a writing session. I spend 5 or so minutes writing about my life, how I am feeling in that moment, or discussing the impact of significant events, and from there springing into whatever creative piece I want to focus on. Alternatively, when under mental duress, I just free write and express all that is on my mind onto the page. Often, this results in a poem or two – and many of the poems shared here and published elsewhere have come from a journaling session.

Consider adding 5 minutes of journaling to your day, and the next time you are overwhelmed, write. Write until you are feeling better and then write some more. Then, that day or at some later stage, read over your words and see if a poem comes, either from the words you have written or inspired by them.

Playing With Perfection

In contrast to 'priming the pump' this time we are going to look at editing a piece of work to 'make it perfect'. The goal being that we are going to take a poem and transform it into the best version of the poem that we can, through a process of editing, refinement, and rewriting. The goal isn't only to make this one poem better, but rather play and practice manipulating our own work, and thus give us more tools and insights when we are writing future work.

Activity – Playing With Perfection

Take any poem you have written over the course of reading this book, or anything you have written in the past. Ideally something that is less than a page long.

During the rest of this activity, I want you to focus both on the technical changes to the poem, but also to the way those changes are making you feel. About the piece and also about yourself.

1: Read the poem out loud. Pause a little bit for a comma, a bit longer for a full stop, and longer still for a line break. Add the appropriate emphasis for any exclamation points or question marks. How does your poem sound to the ear? Are there any changes that need to be made? Save a copy of your unedited poem, and then make those changes.

2: Cut any superfluous words. Can you remove any words from a sentence and still retain the meaning? Consider all instances of 'that' often they can be removed. Consider any uses of 'very', can it and the proceeding word be changed to one stronger word that means the same thing? Make those changes and then repeat part 1 again.

3: Consider your grammar. Would the addition or removal of punctuation like commas, full stops, capital letters, exclamation marks, or questions marks, add to your piece? If so, make those changes and repeat part 1 again.

4: Look at the poem on the page. Is it appealing visually? Are there any tweaks you can make to the line breaks or formatting to make it look good? Make those changes and repeat part 1 again.

5: Compare the original version of the poem with the version you have just been working on. Do you like the changes? Does the poem evoke more emotion/imagery/feel better than the original? Have any core elements been removed that you feel need to be added back in? Make any changes you deem necessary, then repeat this entire process again if you like.

How did you feel during this editing process? Personally, I find that once I get over the shame and self-criticism, I can become 'Editor Zac' and view it from a detached perspective. It is almost as if I am no longer the person who wrote it, but just someone tasked with enhancing the piece to become the best it can be – regardless of who wrote it.

Over time, this exercise will make your writing objectively better. It will show you how and when to cut, and where you can make tweaks to be more evocative. But the greater benefit from this activity comes from the cut to your ego and the detachment from the end result. It will help you to detach yourself from the editing process when writing, and from the writing process when editing. Trust me when I say, that is true creative freedom.

That said, don't forget the 80% adage from an earlier section - Write. Edit. Move on.

Part 5: Worked Examples

A look behind the curtain…

In this section I share the progress that some of my poems took to reach their final form. I will share with you how they originally formed, as well as some of the changes that they went through along the way, finishing with the final form of the poem that I settled on.

When reading, look for changes of phrases, grammar, symbolism, as well as the through lines that last form beginning to end. Note the title choices as well as how each poem is laid out on the page. Ideally, by the end of this section you will realise that all poetry takes time to write, craft, edit, and present, and rarely, if ever, come out perfectly formed off the top of your head.

A Moment That Will Never Come

Attempt 1:

It feels like
I've been preparing
My entire life
For a moment that will never come

My body is tense
My mind is sharp
Yet I have nothing to do

With such focus

There is no enemy to fight
No emergency to survive
No monumental struggle to overcome
Nothing other than this day
And the next and the one after thát

What glory is there to be found
In the daily grind?

How can I be proud of defeating
The mere anxiety of surviving the moment?

Attempt 2:

I crave catastrophe
And ache for the apocalypse

Not as a nihilist
But as a person without purpose

There's little joy to be found in a job
Creating just to consume

Producing just to procreate
Done daily until death

I am man without meaning
Readying myself for revelation

When survival isn't assured life is serious
The useless artefacts will fall away

What actually matters will materialise
Focus will be forced towards functionality

Distracting decadences will be discarded
Leaving nothing but the struggle of life

Perhaps then I'll find real purpose
Maybe existence will feel equanimous

Attempt 3:

How privileged
Am I
To lament
The ease of my life

I am blessed
To have never seen war
Or suffering

I am blessed
Yet that blessing
Feels like a curse of meaning

Without an enemy to fight
Without an obstacle to overcome
All this feels dulled
Life feels like a shadow
A mockery of everything I was promised

Thus I create my own demons
Faceless oppressors
That cannot be seen
Or overcome

Then I cry about my problems
Like they actually exist
Writing angsty poems
From a place of privilege

Final Form:

As a child
I learnt
Vigilance

To survive
I slept light
A knife under my pillow
Waiting for an attack

That attack never came

But I still sleep light
And have made my body into a weapon

I am still vigilant
Waiting for the attack
That will never come

The Cave

Attempt 1:

I wish
I could put aside
My fear
For long enough
To see
To feel
To know
That I am safe

Attempt 2:

I can't enjoy
The moment
Because
I fear
A future

200

That will only
Come
Because my fear
Will stop me from
Doing what is needed
To prevent it
From occurring

Attempt 3:

I cannot
Escape
The echo
Of the words
You never said

I still feel
The ripple
Of the rocks
You dropped
So very long ago

Attempt 4:

My mind
Built itself
A cave
To escape the pain

A silent echo
Reverberates against
The walls
Of my
Inner cave

A place
False solitude
Overlooking
A lake of lies

The ripple
Of the rocks
You dropped
So long ago
Are still moving
Towards the shore

Even so
To this day
When I am afraid
I hide in that cave

Unfortunately
It's no longer a place
Of safety...

But that cave

Is not what it
Once was…

And then you left
First from my life
And then earth…

You never really interacted with me much
So
Formal
So distant
And cold…

I still remember
When I was young
You yelled at me once
I built a cave
Inside my mind
It overlooked a serene lake

A place to
To escape the pain
To escape
You

Final Form:

Once

When I was a young boy
You yelled at me

Objectively
It wasn't much
But it was enough

That night
I built a cave
Inside my mind
One that overlooked
A lake
Whose water
Perfectly reflected
The beauty
Of the nature
That surrounded it

The cave was secret
And strong
And safe

The lake was still
And soft
And serene

I quickly learnt
To hide in that cave
And to gaze upon the water of the lake

Loosing myself
In the reflection
Of a false reality
Made real
By fear

You never yelled at me again
In fact
We never really spoke
At least
Not about anything that mattered

As you pulled away from me
I found solace
Sitting in the cave
Whose creation you inspired

I'd look at the lake
Wishing
You'd appear
Wishing you would
Say
'Son, won't you come swim with me?'

But you never came

Later
When I left home
You didn't fight for me

You didn't speak or even acknowledge
My absence

But you did leave a mark on my mind

That cave
Is now haunted
By the silent screams
Of the words
You left unsaid

And that lake
Still has ripples
From the rocks
We never thew
Together

The beauty of nature is obscured
By your indifference

And
I no longer
Have anywhere safe
To hide

For As Long As I Have Eyes

Unedited Free Writing Session Notes:

00'16"24

Stop trying to write.

No one cares about the latest thought to roll through your head.

About as useful as a tumble weed....

Look at you crafting a narrative

'Oh what Divine skill you have,

Oh what praise you shall receive.'

Bah!

The next thought will be better.

The next thought will suffice.

'Don't look back, only darkness lies beneath.'

Boom. Impactful. A French kiss to your brilliance good sir.

You have enlightened me.

No further instruction needed.

You think *you're* the Messiah?

What about your father, and the man before him?

What about <u>me</u>?

Don't pull back son.

Where would you flee to anyway?

There is no place that is not me.

I am with you always, and in all ways. Even in your doubts of me.

Don't you see? I was that rhyme and the appreciation of it, and the thing appreciating it.

00'16"24
Sixteen seconds of silence is all it took,
For you,
To find me.

Now edit this poem,
Clearly it needs some work ;)

02'58"79
It's not fair for you to be mad at me for not teaching you how to be an artist.
It's a discovery.
It's pain.
It's a journey towards creating your own unique style.
Not to fit a certain look, but because that is the only way you will be able to express yourself.
Don't turn to me for lessons, how could I possibly know you more than you know yourself?
How could I possibly hope to help you express?
You could have seen me.
You could have loved me.
You could have known me.
But all you could see is yourself reflected back by my forced smile.
Given in the same way as it was taken. Interrupted. Confused. Alone.
I dream of flowing lines.
Of black and red reeds painted upon canvas. Dripped

into life.

Pulled forth from my mind. The perfect representation.

The chaos of a moment, captured for eternity.

Or at least as long as I have eyes to see what I've made.

But that vision is a just as much of a lie as these words upon a page.

For they never were written, merely typed. A digital expression of an analogue problem.

I am of two ages.

An alien in both worlds,

none his own,

none his home,

none he wants to return to,

none he wants to live through.

I act and then think.

I act and then justify those actions.

A post hoc self-hypnosis to avoid dissonance. A way to persist. To function.

But to what end?

The answer comes, calling out 'Daddy let me show you something!'.

Final Form:

I dream of flowing lines,

Of black and red reeds painted upon canvas,

Dripped into life,
Pulled forth from my mind,
The perfect representation.
The chaos of a moment
Captured for eternity,
Or at least for as long as I have eyes
To see what I've made.

But that vision
Is a just as much of a lie
As these words upon a page.
For they never were written,
Merely typed.
A digital expression of an analogy problem.

I am of two ages.
An alien in both worlds,
None his own,
None his home,
None he wants to return to,
None he wants to live through.

I act and then think.
I act and then justify those actions.
A post hoc self-hypnosis to avoid dissonance.
A way to persist.
A way to function.

But to what end?

The answer comes
Calling out,
'Daddy let me show you something!'

Part 6: Resources

Taking the next step...

Work With Me

If you would like to take your poetry to the next level and want some personalised guidance, I offer one on one coaching and group workshop sessions. I am also available for online and in person speaking engagements.

Enquires: zachary-phillips.com/coaching

Writing Courses

I also offer a growing collection of writing courses and talks on Skillshare and the Insight Timer app, including the 10-day 'Creative Writing For Healing' audio course, and the 'Poetry For Self-Expression' video course:

insighttimer.com/zacpphillips
sillshare.com/en/user/zacpphillips

Poetry

You can read more of my poetry at zachary-phillips.com/poetry as well as in the following collections:

A Requiem For What Could Have Been, Poetry For The Broken
Augmented Realities, Human Poetry x AI Art
Bound to the Wings of a Butterfly
Can't Quite Express
Kink: Volume 1
Kink: Volume 2
Reflections of the Self, the Poetry, Insights and Wisdom of Silence
Wage Slave: The Unpaid Overtime Edition
Words On A Page, Killing My Inner Demons Through Poetry

Tools

I use the following websites almost daily, favouriting them on my phone for quick access:

Dictionary.com
Howmanysyllables.com
Rhymezone.com
Thesaurus.com

Resources

Below, in alphabetical order, I have listed a collection of books, podcasts, videos, and social media accounts that I have found particularly insightful and instructional:

'Big Magic' - book by Elizabeth Gilbert - An inspirational look at adding creativity into all aspects of your life.

'Collected Love Poems' - poetry by Brian Pattern – A collection of beautiful poetry on the beauty and pain inherent to love.

'Consolations: The Solace, Nourishment and Underlying Meaning of Everyday Words' - book by David Whyte – A novel look at the meaning behind common words, one that has the potential to drastically alter your perceptions.

'Daily Rituals, How Artists Work' - book by Mason Curry – A compilation of the may unique and different ways creative people structure their day, showing you that there is 'no single way' to be creative.

'Hello Future Me' – YouTube Channel – a collection of video essays focusing on the writing process and dissection of what works on the page and on the screen.

'Hip-Hop & Shakespeare? TEDxAldeburgh' – Talk by Akala, a break down of the interconnection between traditional Shakespearian poetry and modern rap.

'How To Read A Poem' - blog post, poets.org - An easy to approach deep dive into how to get the most out of reading poetry.

'Isabelladortapoetry444' – TikTok account – Some of the best spoken word poetry on the internet.

'Let Them Eat Chaos' - - spoken word by Kae Tempest – a modern take on poetry, presented as a blending on spoken word, traditional poetry, and rap.

'Ludovico Einaudi' - musician – lyric less piano based music that I use to assist with my writing.

'Milk and Honey' - poetry by Rupi Kaur – a collection of related poetry that tells a story of pain and recovery.

'Poetry.com' & 'Poetizer.com' – places to read contemporary and classical poetry online.

'Psychological Warfare' – spoken word, by Jocko Willink – If you struggle with procrastination, and need the motivation to sit down and write, listen to this!

'The Alchemist' - book by Paulo Coelho – This popular fable has inspired people all over the world to follow their inner muse, wherever that leads them.

'The Creative Act: A Way Of Being' - book by Rick Rubin – A creative master shares' their findings on the creative process, offering advice and guidance on how to unlock your creativity.

'The Elements Of Style' – book by William Strunk Jr – A well renowned and comprehensive guide to grammar, punctuation, syntax and style.

'The Essential Rumi Revised: New Expanded Edition' - book, collated by Coleman Barks – An amazing collection of poetry from a true master.

'The Laws of Creativity: Unlock Your Originality and Awaken Your Creative Genius' - book by Joey Cofone – Another creative master shares their findings on the creative process, offering advice and guidance on how to unlock your creativity.

'The Name of the Wind' - book by Patrick Rothfuss – A fantasy novel with arguably the best prose out there. Each paragraph is crafted to perfection and the story itself is enjoyable.

'The Prophet' - book by Kahil Gibran – One of the most moving and poignant collections of poetry, loosely crafted into a fictional story.

'The War of Art' - book by Steven Pressfeild – Probably the single best resource to shift all the internal blocks that are stopping you from writing.

'Schnee' – YouTube channel – a collection of video essays on writing, emotion, and character.

'Writing Excuses' - podcast by Brandon Sanderson, Howard Taylor, Dan Wells, Mary Kowal and guests – Advice by some of the greatest writers of our time. Whilst predominantly focusing on fiction, there is a substantial amount of discussion around poetry, the business side of writing, and the creative process in general.

About The Author

Zachary Phillips is a poet, author, and mindset coach. He helps people to take themselves from surviving to passionately thriving using tips, tools, and tricks that enable them to process the past, accept the present, and embrace the future with positivity and purpose.

You can find his writings, podcasts, courses, and coaching via his website: zachary-phillips.com. You can connect with him on social media everywhere @zacpphillips.

Books by Zachary Phillips

Non-Fiction
How To Get Your Sh!t Together
Under The Influence, Reclaiming My Childhood
Mindfulness: A Guidebook to the Present Moment
How To Write Evocative Poetry

Poetry
Requiem For What Could Have Been, Poetry For The Broken
Augmented Realities, Human Poetry x AI Art
Bound To The Wings Of A Butterfly
Can't Quite Express
Reflections Of The Self, The Poetry, Insights, and Wisdom of Silence
Words On A Page, Killing My Inner Demons Through Poetry

Kink: Volume 2

Fiction
Kink: Volume 1
Wage Slave, The Unpaid Overtime Edition
Upgrade